A
LONDON HOME
IN THE
1890s

A
LONDON HOME
IN THE
1890s

M. V. HUGHES

OXFORD NEW YORK MELBOURNE
OXFORD UNIVERSITY PRESS
1978

Oxford University Press, Walton Street, Oxford OX2 6DP

OXFORD LONDON GLASGOW NEW YORK
TORONTO MELBOURNE WELLINGTON CAPE TOWN
IBADAN NAIROBI DAR ES SALAAM
KUALA LUMPUR SINGAPORE JAKARTA HONG KONG TOKYO
DELHI BOMBAY CALCUTTA MADRAS KARACHI

ISBN 0 19 281257 2

First published as *A London Home in the Nineties*,
Part 3 of the trilogy *A London Family 1870–1900*, 1946
First issued as an Oxford Paperback 1978

*Printed in Great Britain by
Fletcher & Son Ltd, Norwich*

CONTENTS

PREFACE

NONE *of the characters in this book are fictitious. The incidents, if not dramatic, are at least genuine memories. Expressions of jollity and enjoyment of life are understatements rather than overstatements. We were just an ordinary, suburban, Victorian family, undistinguished ourselves and unacquainted with distinguished people. It occurred to me to record our doings only because, on looking back, and comparing our lot with that of the children of to-day, we seemed to have been so* lucky. *In writing them down, however, I have come to realize that luck is at one's own disposal, that 'there is nothing either good or bad but thinking makes it so'. Bring up children in the conviction that they are lucky, and behold they are. But in our case high spirits were perhaps inherited, as my story will show.*

> DON PEDRO. *In faith, lady, you have a merry heart.*
> BEATRICE. *Yea, my lord; I thank it, poor fool, it keeps on the windy side of care.*

I

I Cut the Painter

ON the lovely May-day morning of 1890 my mother died,
after an illness of only a few days. Nothing was here
for tears: she had had a remarkably full and exhilarat-
ing life; she had an inborn capacity for casting care aside;
she had always wished for a sudden death; and when she knew
it to be at hand her only request was that I should be good to
her sister Tony.

Now it was to this beloved Cornish aunt of mine that I
owed, almost as much as to my parents, the two best gifts that
any elders can bestow on any children—a happy childhood
and as good an education as lies in their power. So that 'being
good to Tony' involved no burden, but only continuing the
delight of regarding her as a second mother, and spending
part of every holiday with her in Cornwall.

And my mother left me wealthy. In money, no. It was a
case of no work, no dinner. But I was young, healthy, and
doing what I enjoyed. I was teaching in a girls' day-school
in Kensington, under a fine headmistress, who allowed me to
work along the lines I liked. Also I had three elder brothers,
of whom I could never determine which was the most loved.
Unfortunately, they were not at hand; the eldest, Tom, was
living in Yorkshire with wife and children; the second, Dym,
was more mobile as a bachelor, and was teaching mathematics
in a school in Plymouth (a place on the way to Cornwall!);
and the third, Barnholt, was at sea. These three would be
bulwarks for me all through life, as mother was well aware,
but she had been accustomed to ejaculate occasionally, 'If only
I saw you married to a good man I should die happy'. Well,
she died quite at rest on that point, for on my twenty-first
birthday I had become engaged to the man of all others that

she admired most. This was Arthur Hughes, who, like Dym, was teaching mathematics. But, unlike Dym, he hated the work, and was reading for the Bar, not as an escape, but because the Law, even in its seemingly absurd intricacies, fascinated him. His work was at Bedford, and I saw something of him once a fortnight when he came up to Gray's Inn to 'eat his dinners'.

In spite of all these sources of wealth, I was desolate. A mother's death must always make one feel cut away at the roots, and in my case it was worse, because she had always been like a sister as well as a mother in her complete comradeship and youthful outlook. My brother Dym, whom she and I used to call 'the branch of our family at Plymouth', was well aware how badly I felt her loss, and came to the rescue by frequent letters and an occasional dash up to Kensington, to see me and take me out somewhere. As soon as the summer term was over he insisted on my spending a week with him on Dartmoor, where he and his friend Barber were as usual to be trout-fishing. He met me at Newton Abbot and took me on to Totnes for a day or two, where we could have some walks beside the broad waters of the Dart. I enjoyed the scenery and the walks enormously, but what bothered Dym was that I had no appetite, even after a long walk. I was really sorry about this, for he tried to tempt me with all he could think of. I remember his astonished cry, 'What! Not eat this salmon! Why, my dear child, it was in the Dart a few hours ago!' 'Oh, Dym,' I pleaded, 'I really would if I could.' 'Well, darling,' said he, 'we'll see what a drive over the moor will do for you to-morrow.'

The air on that glorious drive blew away my lassitude. I took off my hat and let the wind do what it liked with my close-cropped hair. I laughed as I hadn't laughed for many weeks, from sheer physical exhilaration, and I felt like a newly created being as we drew up at the Duchy Hotel, Princetown. Dym had mentioned our destination, and both town and hotel sounded very grand to me. Indeed I felt a little nervous about the small size of my bag, at which Dym had raised an eyebrow when he met me at Newton Abbot. But I was reassured on our arrival, for of town I saw none at all, and the hotel was surprisingly modest in appearance. To Dym it had become, from his frequent holidays spent there, almost a second home, and the proprietress welcomed us warmly. I soon found that the simplicity of the hotel was entirely confined to the things that didn't matter—its architecture and interior furnishings. Bedrooms and sitting-rooms were bare and even ugly, but the ducal quality of the hotel shone forth in its meals. These quite staggered me in their munificence. But I was prepared to justify them. How Dym laughed as he watched me dealing with the dinner after our arrival. The wind and sun of the moor had burnt my cheeks and sharpened my appetite to a quite inelegant extent; and not only Barber and his wife, but the other visitors too, couldn't help smiling. For this was one of those rare hotels (so rare that in a wide experience I have never come across another) where English people look cheerfully at all their fellow guests, and speak on the slightest provocation or none.

The meals were peculiar in another way. They faded out in the middle of the day. In fact the whole hotel faded out. After giving us a colossal breakfast, including real ham, fish, new-laid eggs, chops and steaks, raspberries and bilberries, and bowls of clotted cream at decent intervals on the table, the entire staff disappeared. I imagined that they went into contemplation on the subject of evening dinner for some hours, and then it was all hands to the task of creating it. Such degrading trifles as lunch and tea were nothing accounted of. Mrs. Barber and I were the only female guests, and the men were all there for outdoor sport of some kind. I don't know about the others, but Dym used to go the whole day between breakfast and dinner without opening his mouth, either to put anything in or utter a word. He and Barber would set off for the stream, the upper reaches of the Dart, lost to everything except trout, for they designedly fished well apart so as not to interfere with each other's sport.

Meanwhile, Mrs. Barber and I knew our role quite well:

we had the freedom of the moor, but must on no account come near the fishermen lest we disturb the trout, who (so the men asserted) had a rooted objection to womenfolk. Not far from the hotel was a tiny shop, the village Whiteley we called it, for it was so full of oddments of universal provision that it was difficult to edge into it. Indeed, there was a little home-made notice pinned by the door, 'Please enter sideways'. We suspected that this had been put there by some wag in the hotel. Here we would capture every morning a few biscuits or apples or nuts to take with us on our wanderings about the moor. We also took books, but I read very little, liking rather to bask in the sun and give myself up to the uncanny fascination of the boundless moor. The time passed rapidly, and we didn't even pine for a cup of tea at four o'clock, but weren't we all ready for our evening dinner!

The Barbers had to leave the day before we did, and Dym decided, in spite of my protests, that he wouldn't leave me alone all day. 'You've really seen very little of the moor,' said he, 'we'll spend our last day in going for a drive, so that you will be able to see more than you can by walking. The trout will be glad if I lay off a bit.' So he hired a pony-trap and off we started. It was the smallest little two-wheeled carriage imaginable. I think it must have been designed to carry one good-sized man, perhaps a farmer, to market. As we were both of small make we managed to sit squeezed together on the high seat. The pony was fresh and seemed to enjoy scudding at a spanking pace along the white tracks of road that could be seen winding away miles ahead. There were no hedges to hide them, but now and again the track would disappear in a dip of the moor, to reappear some distance farther on. Here and there would come a fork, and Dym, who knew the moor like the palm of his hand, never hesitated at such a junction. He was making for one or two favourite spots to show me, and I couldn't help wondering how he could tell one road from another without hedges or trees or any landmark whatever.

'I shouldn't care to be dropped here to find my way back,' said I, after an hour of this kind of thing.

'No, nor any one else who doesn't know the moor. For a stranger it's the very dickens. I'm always sorry for those poor chaps who try to escape their warders. I'll show you some of them on our way back, working in a gang.'

'What do they work at?'

'Mostly low stone hedges where no hedges are wanted. I think they might be given something to do that's worth while. The absurd little walls are built very slowly and beautifully, because they've more time than they know what to do with. I suppose the uselessness is part of the punishment. I've heard it said that the severest torture you can inflict on a man is to make him upset a load of stones, fill the cart again, unload them again, and so on. But it seems to me that the long term is enough without any torture at all.'

'Do you ever speak to the poor fellows?'

'No, strictly forbidden. Nor give them anything. But often when I've passed near enough to catch the eye of one of them I've dropped some baccy accidentally.'

When we had been driving for two hours or more, only stopping now and again to enjoy the view of some special tor, we reached what seemed a metropolis after the desert moorland, for we had not met a single person. Here there was actually a post-office and one or two cottages.

'You can guess the name of this place,' said Dym, 'for here's the post-office and here's the bridge—Postbridge.'

He hitched up the pony, and we were glad to get out and stretch our legs a bit. A river always drew Dym like a magnet and we hung over the bridge and stared at the water. The sun was shining brilliantly, showing up all the beauties of the moor and sky, for there were great masses of white clouds, and fleeting shadows on the middle-distance downlands. It was a perfect day, and I had no mind to leave Postbridge. But Dym descried a cloud no bigger than a man's hand, of a kind quite different from the white ones. Making a rapid reckoning of the way of the wind, the time, and the distance from home, he thought we could get back before the cloud began business. But he thought we had better be starting, because you never knew on Dartmoor when you might be overtaken by a sudden squall and be drenched before you knew where you were. That would be nothing, I thought, for I should never know where I was anyway. We squeezed in again and turned the pony towards home. As we went Dym regaled me with the story of two men who were caught in a sudden downpour on the moor. There was, of course, no shelter of any kind, no symptom of hedge or bush anywhere. One of the men, an old *habitué*, saw the storm coming, hunted round for a good-sized stone, stripped off all his clothes and pushed them under the stone just in time. Down came the rain and he skipped about in it cheerfully. 'You fool!' cried the other, 'You'll catch your death,' as he huddled himself together as well as he could, but was getting drenched to the skin. In a few minutes the shower was over, out blazed the sun again, and the old hand continued his physical exercises till he was dry, then pulled out his dry clothes and put them on, with 'Who's the fool now?'

While we were laughing over this we saw that our own cloud was ominously near. The pony seemed to sense it, too, and hardly needed a touch of the whip to put out at his best pace; but the rain was upon us, a real searching pour, and we went into the 'Duchy' like drowned rats.

'Never mind,' said Dym, 'it's just the luck of the moor, and our laughter has kept us from catching cold—there's nothing like being jolly for warding off things. We'll just change and be as right as a trivet.'

'Change!' thought I, as I went up to my room, 'that is exactly what I cannot do,' and I looked ruefully at the few belongings which I had spread about on my arrival, to make them appear as many as possible in the various drawers and cupboards. I might just as well have looked out of the window for any possible garment. So I went to Dym's room and tapped at the door.

'I say, Dym, don't be shocked, but I've nothing to change *into*.'

'What! You have come to Dartmoor with only one dress!

Well, that beats cock-fighting, as mother used to say. . . . I'll see what the proprietress can do—she's equal to most emergencies.'

She was all smiles and accommodation, with a cheering undertone of approval . . . 'and quite right, my dear, not to come to a country place like this with a lot of fal-lals.' She produced a black silk dress, doubtless her Sunday one, and carried off my wet one to be dried by the kitchen fire. As she was nearly twice my size I added greatly to the gaiety of the dinner-table by hobbling in and gathering the folds as I went. So I needn't have been distressed, for it provided a jolly finale to a supremely happy week.

The next day we were off to Cornwall, to stay with our numerous relations in Camborne. Here Dym indulged me in my passion for riding by taking me for canters along the cliffs, on the grassy track that stretched for miles between the sea and the heather; and sometimes we would go farther afield to one of those Cornish villages with entrancing names. Tony encouraged the idea by having a beautiful new habit made for me. I felt very grand walking up to the horse in my trousers, with the tail of my skirt flung over my arm and flicking my crop. But that long skirt and that clumsy side-saddle—how ridiculous and dangerous they seem now! And when I see the modern girls in their sensible trousers, sitting safely and comfortably astride, I wish my riding days were not past. To have a horse under one gives an intoxication that the best bicycle or even the fastest car cannot inspire. Even an aeroplane has its limits; it can't give one companionship, it can never be a Pegasus.

One of the excursions that Dym planned stands vividly in my memory. It was a glorious summer morning and we started off to Helston, an old town full of historic and romantic associations for all Cornish people—especially the Furry Dance in May, one of the real pagan relics of the Phoenician Baal worship that has not been stamped out by the Wesleyan conscience. Our objective was a little farther on—Porthleven, on Mount's Bay. There we put up our horses at the inn and enjoyed a mighty lunch.

'Let's go for a stroll by the sea,' said Dym, 'I've got something funny to show you.'

And indeed it was one of the oddest natural formations I ever saw. The river Cober rises some ten miles north of Mount's Bay, fully intending to flow respectably into it; but just as it gets a few yards from the sea it receives a rude check; the sea seems to say, 'We don't want you,' and puts up a sand-bar, called the Loo. So the river has quite contentedly, as though with a smile, broadened out into a lake. Dym had often fished in this Loo Pool, so he knew it well, but was delighted at my staring at it in perplexity. At our backs, as we stood on the sand-bar, was the restless Atlantic, and in front of us a lovely expanse of perfectly calm water, with masses of beautiful trees coming down to its edge and waterfowl swooping over it. Dym's thoughts were not with the beauty of the scene, but with the trout that were escaping being caught, and as he grew lyrical over these I reflected how jolly it was of him to give up a day's fishing merely to take me to a place that he knew well. But I think my excitement and enjoyment of every moment till we reached home in the dusk made him as happy as myself.

It was on that ride home that he seized the chance to approach a subject that was on his mind. Our horses, a bit tired, were going at a walking pace.

'You know, Molly dear, I think Arthur is a splendid fellow —the best in the world—but I feel responsible for you now, and I can't let you be married until he has some kind of settled income. It seems a bit mad to me, this reading for the Bar.'

'But he loves it, Dym, and he is sick of teaching mathematics, and I would much rather wait till he gets the work he enjoys doing.'

'Yes, but the Bar is so precarious at any time, even if you have influence, which Arthur hasn't.'

'I know, but it's more fun to do things off your own bat, even if you don't make so much money.'

'You're as bad as mother. She never knew or cared what her income was, if income it could be called.'

It amused me to remember this conversation a year or two

later, when Dym himself was engaged to be married. He wrote to me, 'I don't hold with all this waiting; it's much better to be married and chance it.' That was all very well for him, but he was not intending to change his profession, as Arthur was. In fact, Arthur was taking big risks, for he was struggling with greater difficulties than Dym or I were aware of at the time. I knew that his mother lived alone in Wales, and relied on him to look after her, but it was not until many years later that I had a glimpse of those anxious years of which he never spoke. One of the oldest of his innumerable friends wrote to me about him, and after quoting Tacitus' *Suorum memor, sui negligens,* he went on: 'What a gallant fight he put up all his life against time and tide and fate and difficulties. He never had a proper chance. Lack of money clogged his steps at Cambridge . . . but he was eager to give it to others, and to my certain knowledge, when he was teaching at Bedford, nearly half his meagre salary went in alms to his "doctor brother" and "parson brother". His extraordinary capacity for making friends went alongside with fiery indignation at anything mean. "On bad terms with Paterson?" he burst out once to some would-be peace-maker. "Of course I am. I should be ashamed of myself if I were *not* on bad terms with Paterson."'

My mother used to call him Don Quixote, the greatest compliment she could bestow on any one. And indeed the parallel was fairly close, for he was always ready to go to any length for any one in trouble, and give or lend as much as he could. I think I was the only one who never came in for his indulgence, for he was as severe with me as he was with himself. I had become so much a part of himself that I seemed to be included in Tacitus' *sui.* The realization of this afforded me deep satisfaction, for I felt that I had something that the ordinary love-story didn't know about.

§ 2

Our poor financial prospects had induced me to do my utmost to save a little money, and I had been working hard to get my degree to improve my market value. I had already taken the Intermediate B.A. and was in the thick of preparing for the Final when mother died. She had taken the most intimate interest in every subject, and for some time after her death I could hardly bear the look of the books. But my holiday in Devon and Cornwall put new life into me and I was able to get through the Final in the autumn. My headmistress, who was one of the best, was very pleased, gave me more responsibility, and raised my salary.

All would have been well had it not been for my so-called home conditions. My post was a non-resident one, and I could have lived where I liked, but mother and I and a fellow teacher, Miss Williamson, had consented (much against the grain) to live at a house that had been started to accommodate a few pupils of the school who wanted to be boarders—just to help the scheme along. As long as mother's jolly presence enlivened the household it was bearable enough, but it was badly run, and the pupils who wanted to board there began to dwindle. Soon a quite different type of boarder was imported—several music students. There may be worse companions than music students, but, if so, I have yet to meet them. Singly, and for occasional social intercourse, they are probably delightful, but to live with in bulk! It was, of course, to their credit that they practised, but there was no close time for it. Practice, instrumental and vocal, would go on·at any hour, frequently simultaneously in separate rooms, and the performers were never *all* out of the house at the same time. One advantage I gained from this was a lifelong ability to work through any noise. Worse than the practising nuisance was the talk at meal-times. Music must surely be an elevating business, but it seemed to have left these students untouched. Their conversation consisted almost exclusively of gossip and low jokes about the masters at the Academy of Music. If it's really funny I can enjoy a low joke with the best, but these were entirely humourless, and Miss Williamson and I didn't 'hear' them. Our failure to be shocked annoyed the tellers and spurred them to fresh efforts. Oddly enough it never occurred to us that we might go to live somewhere else, but we escaped from that house whenever we could, and as soon as my examination was over I had more time for outings.

Seeing one day by chance that *Much Ado* was on at the Lyceum, I was seized by the idea that it would be fun to go to see it. The main attraction was that mother had always loved that play, chiefly the gaiety of Beatrice and the absurdity of Dogberry. 'But oh, you should see it *acted*', she would add. I had never inquired where she herself had seen it, and wish now that I knew what famous actors had made the play live for her. Another attraction for me was the Lyceum and Irving. From childhood I had heard enough of Irving from my brother Charles to arouse the keenest expectation, so that to see him in *Much Ado* would be a link with both him and mother. All this about a visit to the theatre! Well, at the age of twenty-four I had been to a play only some half-dozen times, and in each case I had been taken by a brother who managed it all. Was it possible, I wondered, to arrange such an outing without being 'taken'? I approached Miss Williamson. Did she think that we might venture together one Friday night when there would be no school the next day? She did most decidedly, and when we saw that we could go there and back by omnibus, and that the gallery was only a shilling, we hesitated no longer.

It was like tasting blood, or some exciting drug, for our first experience was so delightful that we missed no play that Irving put on, and as he was giving a rotation of them we were able to see something different nearly every week. But it was an endurance test, and I can quite understand why it was usual in those days for a girl to be 'taken' to a theatre. To get anything like a good seat in the gallery (and we could afford no better) we had to be there at least two hours before the doors opened. This meant standing on the stone staircase, which was lit here and there by a gas-jet in a wire cage, and smelt of orange-peel and stale perspiration. The light wasn't good enough to read by, so we amused ourselves by talking over the play and watching the human nature surging around us.

As soon as the glad sound of the pushing of a bolt told us that the doors were being opened, the insidious gentle pushing that had been going on all the time became less gentle, and we had to use our elbows to avoid being crushed, and sometimes a group of youths would make a concerted rush. . . . How glad we were to get past the paying-barrier and be free to leap ahead. Then followed a race, as we jumped over the low benches to reach the front row. There were no backs to the seats or divisions between them, so we were thankful to find ourselves in front of a kindly woman who would let us lean against her knee. In those days of gas-lighting and poor ventilation the atmosphere of the gallery didn't bear thinking about. But all discomforts were forgotten as soon as the curtain went up.

Among the plays we saw I best remember these: *The Bells*, *The Lyons Mail*, *The Corsican Brothers*, *Olivia* (an adaptation of *The Vicar of Wakefield*), *Charles I*, and, above all, *Much Ado*, which we saw three times. Ellen Terry was Beatrice as one might always imagine her, a mixture of impishness and deep feeling, from the moment when the play springs to life with her 'I wonder you will still be talking, Signior Benedick; nobody marks you', right through till her lightning flash 'Kill Claudio' is followed by Benedick's thunder-clap reply. Surely no two lovers were more interesting. Most of the people around us seemed ignorant of the story and engrossed in its development. In the one tantalizingly short love-scene, interrupted by Beatrice's being summoned to her uncle, a woman behind me exclaimed, 'Oh, bother the uncle!'

In this play, too, Irving was at his best, for he knew how to bring out the humour of Benedick by a score of little gestures and facial expressions. In his tragic roles I was fascinated by the curious drag of the leg—a trait that Charles used to imitate with great effect. But on looking back I get little pleasure in retrospect from his treatment of tragedy, and even at the time much of it seemed exaggerated, and even ridiculous. The worst was *Lear*. In this Irving was so doddering and silly to begin with that he left no room to get much madder, and his wild efforts at it were so tiresome that when he fell asleep in the hut it was a sheer relief, and I nearly called out to Edgar, 'Don't wake him.'

It is difficult to imagine Irving playing the part of Jingle— a not only farcical but subsidiary role. Yet Arthur actually saw this and said it was one of the funniest things he had ever seen on the stage. He was convinced that Irving's real genius lay in acting comic parts and that it was his itch to play Hamlet that had been his undoing.

These excursions cost little, considering the amount of pleasure we got from them, for eighteenpence usually covered our expenses. However, there was another indulgence that I allowed myself as a rare treat. Of this I was rather ashamed, and kept it quiet. Ever since my childhood a ride in a hansom had been a thing of bliss, and it still held some quality of fairy-land for me. With a half-crown to waste I would walk along Kensington High Street, eyeing the crawlers, as the empty cabs were called. Drivers, expectant, would hold up a whip hopefully as I looked about. But I waited till I had seen a cab with all the right points : india-rubber tyres, good horse, cheery-looking cabby with a grey top hat and a flower in his button-hole. Then my raised finger was enough to bring him up to my side. In a blasé voice I would mention some entrancing spot as a destination, such as the Abbey, or Romano's. The reins would be elegantly lifted for me to get in, and I would sit back and float away, enjoying the London streets as Provi-dence intended them to be enjoyed. Reaching my destina-tion I would quietly return by omnibus. I liked to choose a restaurant for the cab to put me down, because of a story my brother Charles told me. As he was strolling along Oxford Street one evening a cabby drew up and said to him, 'Going to the Cri, Sir? I'll take you there for nothing.' When Charles looked surprised he added in an undertone, 'We aren't allowed to crawl there, but if we drive up with a fare, we are bound to get another.' 'Right,' said Charles, got in, and as he jumped out at the Criterion pretended to pay a fare to the grateful cabby.

So often has it seemed to happen in my life that the worst things have been fruitful of the best, and here was an instance.

The disagreeable conditions of our boarding-house drove us to the real enlargement of life that the theatre gave us. And on summer afternoons they drove us to long country walks, to Richmond Park or to Kew Gardens. We used to start forth by a tram, whose progress along the single line was so slow, with stops for change of passengers and long waits on loop lines for another tram to pass, that once I remember being disgusted to notice that a hay-cart with its steady plod was actually gaining on us. But, as in the gallery, when we reached the Gardens all tedium was forgotten, and we made for the Arboretum and spent happy hours stretched under the trees, reading and talking.

It was on one of our reluctant journeys back to the hated boarding-house that Miss Williamson made the bold suggestion that we should break loose and set up in rooms by ourselves. Taking fire at this, I made the bolder suggestion that we should make a completely fresh start by looking for new posts. 'Well, *you* begin,' said Miss Williamson, and urged me on before I had time to cool. So that same evening I went round to our headmistress, Miss Bennett, broached the idea and asked her advice. She was certainly taken aback, but was most generous in manner and deed, pressing upon me that it was time I took a post with wider scope than she could offer me, and promising me all the backing-up she could give.

'Let me see, how old are you now?'

'I'm twenty-four, but I don't feel like it.'

'Quite time you made a change. And don't mind me, dear. I shall write to the Cambridge Training College and ask Miss Hughes to send me another Miss Thomas.'

So kind was she that I returned in the mood to give up all idea of leaving her. But Miss Williamson kept me up to the mark, thrust note-paper at me, and advised me to write at once to my old school, the North London Collegiate, to see whether I could get a post there. So I appealed to my ever-revered friend, Mrs. Bryant, ran out with my letter, and dropped it in the pillar-box with that rubicon feeling one often experiences at these little red perils.

II

A New Venture

§ 1

'COME and see me to-morrow.'

This was the tantalizing reply to my letter. I started for Camden Town in the afternoon, telling myself not to hope for anything immediate. It was probably only to be a visit of friendly interest and promise for the future. But it was with real eagerness added to her wonted affection that Mrs. Bryant received me. Speaking hurriedly she told me that on getting my letter she had intended to give me a post in the school, but that something odd had just happened. Shortly before my arrival there had rushed upon her a member of the Council of Bedford College, full of a scheme for opening a training department for teachers, as a branch of the College. Their students, who were intending to teach, either started without any training or were going off to Cambridge for it. 'She seemed a bit incoherent,' said Mrs. Bryant, 'but clearly the main obstacle is the difficulty of finding any one who can undertake to run the scheme, and she hoped that I might know of some one. So I told her that I had got the very one that would do, actually wanting new work, and coming to see me, and I promised to send you on to her as soon as you came.' 'Me!' I gasped. 'Yes, you, and don't stop to talk but run down the road after her, towards the station. She's very tall and big, and dressed in black. Run.'

I ran, and soon saw my quarry nearing the station. She seemed very pleased when I touched her arm and said that I had been sent by Mrs. Bryant. Confused as I had been by Mrs. Bryant, I was still more so by the vague ideas poured forth on me as the Camden Road trams went by, but I gathered that the College was in London, not Bedford (as I had imagined), that the new work would not begin for some months, that I must send in some testimonials, and come for an interview later in the year. It all seemed a nice long time off, so I readily agreed, half hoping that some other candidate for the post would be preferred. However, I set about gathering some testimonials. Miss E. P. Hughes, of Cambridge, sent me a splendid one, but added that she hoped I wouldn't get the post as she wanted me to come to Cambridge as her vice-principal.

I know now that there was no other candidate on the horizon, but the appearance of 'appointment' and 'choice' had to be gone through, and in the autumn term I was summoned to Bedford College for an interview. It was a murky afternoon when I reached York Place, Baker Street, precisely at the appointed hour of 3.30. Councils are like dentists, far too dignified to receive the poor wretch at the actual time named, and I was shown into a kind of large office to wait. I was in the best possible condition for the ordeal, since I didn't care a rap whether they appointed me or not. Also I had a splitting headache which checked my usual tendency to smile, and lent me a temporary dignity. Presently a dear old lady in a cap (whom I discovered later to be the Principal) sailed in with a cup of tea for me. She belonged to that incredible period of women's education when an older lady of some kind, either the Principal or a 'Lady Visitor', had to sit through lectures given by male professors, as a chaperone. Sharp criticism by a young professor, of a poor answer or essay, would often un-nerve a girl and reduce her to tears; so the Lady Visitor was present to prevent such a break-down, or to calm the student with smelling-salts.

'Don't you be nervous, dear,' said this kind Principal in an undertone, as she ushered me into the large board-room.

There, seated at a vast round table, were the Council— about a dozen men and women of mature age. In full view of them all, at the respectful distance of a yard from the table, a chair had been pulled out for me. What with the cup of tea and my don't-care mood, I felt completely mistress of the situation and very soon sensed that it was the Council who were worried, having not the faintest idea what my work was to be and what intelligent questions they could put to me. 'This is a very anxious and responsible undertaking, is it not?' was the general tone of the chairman and several other kindly men, and to all these noble thoughts I assented freely. But there was one old woman waiting her chance and crouching to spring. I have never seen any one so ugly in face, so repellent in manner. She had a constant feud (as I learnt afterwards) with the member of the Council who had originated this idea of a Training Department, and had prepared herself to damn it if possible. As soon as the men had exhausted their rather point-less questions, she took the floor. Eyeing me fiercely, she opened her speech with the statement that she had personally inspected this so-called training work. Then she described with vivid detail, diverting illustrations, and great relish, the unpractical rubbish that went on, the outrageous nonsense that was being taught, and the utter waste of time of the whole concern. When she had used up all her facts and epithets, she sat back and glared, pausing for a reply. Meanwhile I had had leisure to note the embarrassment of the other members, and the uncomfortable fidgeting of the men at her bullying rude-ness. So I looked at her dreamily for a moment or two in silence, and then said slowly: 'You seem to have had a very narrow, and a very unfortunate experience of training work.'

An outbreak of scarcely checked delight rippled round the assembly, and to cover the awkwardness the kindly chairman made some pleasant and non-committal remarks to me, and I was allowed to depart without further question. A few days later I received notice that I was appointed, and that I was to begin work in the following January. It was a blow to find that for this 'anxious and responsible undertaking' I was to receive £100, non-resident. Even in those days, when money went farther than it does to-day, it was almost a starvation salary. Cambridge would be far better than this, thought I, and I wrote to the Bedford College authorities to this effect, pointing out that Miss Hughes was anxious to have me. But I had such an indignant letter from the member who had started the scheme, accusing me of breaking my promise to her, that I gave way to her insistence, although I knew perfectly well that I had made no promise at all. She admitted then that I had been the only candidate for the post, and I thought she might have appealed to me more suitably than by accusing me of perfidy. But she was too masterful to be gainsaid, and I comforted myself with the reflection that though I should have little money I should have an absolutely free hand to do what I liked.

All my spare time was now spent in planning my campaign. My students were presumed to have had a good education, with a degree or other qualification, and required only professional training for one year. In other words, I could assume that they knew the subject they were to teach, and only needed to be helped to teach it effectively and to see its relation to education as a whole. Even this vague idea was not suggested to me by Bedford College authorities, who left me to do exactly as I liked. Even my men friends, my 'pillars' in all emergencies, my brothers and Arthur, didn't seem likely to be much use here. To Tom and Dym the training of a teacher seemed merely funny. But a holiday spent at Arthur's home in Aberdovey enabled me to pin him down for help. 'Well,' said he, 'the great thing for whatever you set about, is to start with a skeleton.' 'Oh I've got my skeleton,' said I, 'it's this: first term, some simple psychology in very close relation to actual lessons; second term, special school subjects; third term, bigger educational problems. Then I've got to edge in some hygiene, some logic, and some history of great educators.'

Arthur approached my scheme in a sceptical spirit. He shook his head over psychology as being only a grand name for common sense. 'As for boys,' said he, 'there's nothing like a good caning all round on a Monday morning, whether they deserve it or not. It steadies them.' But he was willing to admit that the teachers of girls might possibly attain some common sense by means of a little logic and psychology, if the lectures were kept practical. Glancing at my third-term programme he said: 'Don't be too nebulous about what you call bigger educational problems. Why not give them some hard facts?' 'What do you suggest?' I asked. 'What about a course on Educational Polity?' 'Polity? Is that the same as policy?' 'No, there's a big distinction; the policy of a society is its relation to other societies, but its polity is its management of its own affairs. It would be good for these girls to know something of the development of education in England during the nineteenth century, the effects of the industrial revolution on it, and all that kind of thing.'

'Did that affect education much?' I asked.

'Yes. People got drunk with the idea of producing large quantities of things cheaply, such as iron railings, and they thought that masses of children could be educated by similar cheap methods. Hence the curse of making them sit in rows, "being good", while one teacher spouts at them or insists on their all doing the same exercise. If your students see the origin of this, they will no longer consider it a method ordained by providence, or even a practical necessity. And if you know how a thing grew up you are half-way to seeing how to improve it.'

This sounded good, but I didn't know where to turn for the facts. 'Oh, I can give you the main ones,' said Arthur, and then and there began to reel out to me descriptions of the old hedge-schools and dame schools, the 'inventions' of Bell and Lancaster to meet the demand for 'mass' instruction by means of monitors, the founding of the National and British Societies, and so on to Forster's Bill in 1870 and compulsory education for all. It took us many a seance to cover all this ground, and I was busy taking notes all the time. Comparison of our polity with those of France and Germany had to be discussed, as well as the status of the so-called public schools, the universities, and private schools. Then, of course, the religious question (a serious bone of contention in Wales) was considered, and the difficult point as to whether education, if compulsory, ought not also to be free. I felt provided with ample matter for a short course on these lines for my third term.

'How did you come to know all this?' I asked.

'A man gets to know these things,' said he.

A married friend to whom I related this incident with some pride was not at all impressed. 'That's the usual thing, Molly,' said she. 'One of the great advantages of being married you will soon find is that you have a fount of wisdom ever springing at your side; you have only to dip. How men get to know everything astounds me. And it's the same thing if something goes wrong in the house—a clock won't go, a tap drips, or there's a smell of gas—as soon as the wretched thing sees a pair of trousers it gives up the game and resumes work.'

'A bit humiliating for us, isn't it?' said I.

'Not at all. We women have far more difficult and delicate problems to face. If we were learned and practical and wise we should have no reserve strength.'

§ 2

On the opening morning in January 1892 I walked into the lecture-room that had been assigned to me, feeling a fair amount of confidence. But two shocks awaited me. The students were duly there, looking all pleasant and expectant, but seated firmly on one side, note-book in hand, was the member of the Council who had sponsored the new department. She had come, she said, to see how I should start it. My plan was to devote the first hour to giving my skeleton of the year's work, with reasons for this and that. I soon gathered from her manner that my visitor was properly impressed, and at the close she was very cordial in her appreciation of the scheme. I fancy that she was anxious to be prepared against any attacks from her enemy on the Council.

The other shock was to see, sitting meekly among my students, none other than Miss Armstead, the classics mistress of the North London Collegiate School, who was the finest teacher I had ever sat under. She smiled happily at me now and again during that first hour, but as soon as possible I approached her in the spirit of John the Baptist, to ask why on earth she had come to me for help in a business at which she herself was so brilliant. 'Oh, I know absolutely nothing about psychology,' said she, 'nor logic nor hygiene nor all these other things you mention. It's all so exciting. . . . My only regret is that I shan't be able to attend full time, because of my work at school. And I shan't be able to do any of the practical work. What fun it will be just to go about theorizing, when I've been making mistakes all my life!'

I was relieved that she didn't want practical work, for that was my chief trouble. All theorizing might be fun, but it was not my idea of training. I wanted, if it could be managed, that every psychological law mentioned should be illustrated in school life; and that every success or failure in school life should be explained by a psychological law. But to get school life—that was the rub. The College authorities made not the slightest effort to help me in this matter by giving me introductions to the schools in the neighbourhood. I had to go round and beg for permission to give a few lessons here and there. I was as coldly received as if I were attempting to sell tea or basket-chairs. Then, of course, I was told that training was entirely useless, or indeed harmful—'putting ideas into their heads'; that having strangers in upset the school routine; and so on. I admitted all. Then, by throwing myself on their mercy, and by pointing out how enhanced would be their chances of heaven if they helped the cause of education by giving me half an hour a week, I induced one or two kindly disposed principals to allow us in on trial. One of the schools to which I gained admission was a little dame's school, where Mangnall's *Questions* were actually in use. With my scanty triumphs I returned to College and parcelled out among the students the few courses available, so as to squeeze the utmost value from these scraps of real teaching. Syllabuses were prepared for them, notes for each lesson considered, and friendly discussions (rather than formal criticisms) carried out in College afterwards. As time went on and downright failures were few, and the schools survived the dangerous outside influence, and the pupils received us with delight, and the teachers got a spare half-hour for their corrections . . . why even the principals became pleasant, and actually tried to be helpful. One day I was drawn aside privily by the headmistress for her to impart her new-born idea: 'What these students really need is to be shown *how* to teach.' I smiled assent and admitted that her advice was sound.

Another difficulty had been lurking in my mind for a long time, and as the second term was coming near I had to face it. How best to deal with special subjects? Each student would probably intend to specialize in some branch, such as mathematics, modern languages, or science. Jack of all trades though I was, it was not possible for me to cope with the best methods for all these. Suddenly I realized that I was starving in the midst of plenty. Bedford College was replete with professors of everything, genial fellows with whom I had hobnobbed at staff meetings. Surely I could harness them. So one by one I waylaid them in some passage and asked them casually whether they would spare an hour to give my students a lecture on their subject.

'But what on earth is there to say about it?' was the usual tone of the reply.

'You must find among your own students some who have been badly taught?'

'Oh, rather!'

'Well then, just come and talk to my people about your grievances, tell them how you wish all schoolchildren could be properly taught your subject, what mistakes to avoid, what chief points to aim at, and so on. Or indeed talk about anything at all. It is the clash with a bigger mind that these girls want, especially a man's, for they may be buried in girls' schools for years. I don't care what revolutionary ideas you put into their heads—in politics or religion or art—so long as you say what you really mean.'

As I pressed my point in such ways a look of intelligence would come over my victim's face, and he would beamingly agree to do his best, and fix a date. My plan was to devote a complete week to each leading school subject. Before the lecture was to be given the College library was raided for any books on the subject, various text-books were produced and criticized, our own past troubles were discussed, and the latest modern methods were soberly considered. We had plenty of questions to propound to the lecturer when his hour arrived. And what good stuff each professor gave us, evidently enjoying the chance to say what he thought, letting loose subversive views in an irresponsible way, abusing ancient follies and modern fads.

The most revolutionary was the history specialist, Mr. Allen, who was so earnest that he twisted himself into a kind of knot round his chair and barked out his opinions like a Hyde Park orator. He was dead against all the usual methods of teaching history, training his biggest guns against any attempt to draw morals or any effort to make it picturesque. Science, that was the thing. History was merely a branch of biology. The doings of human beings in the past were to be studied and recorded as cold-bloodedly as the wrigglings of insects under the microscope. The students were too much overawed to ask him how this method was to be carried on in school life, but they were wholesomely headed off anything like an emotional touch in their history lessons.

The mathematics man was generous indeed, not only in his ready assent to my request, but also in his offer to give a series of six talks. One would not be of much use, he said, for it was in the earliest stages of dealing with Number that the mischief began, and he would like to talk about those difficulties as well as the later ones. 'I find that my women students here in College cannot be broken of their school habit of shirking fresh thought, and waiting for some "rule" or "dodge" and then learning it by heart; real grappling with a problem has become almost impossible for them. People ought to begin with realities in the cradle.' Mr. Harding was a man of humour as well as sympathy with weakness, and his talks were enjoyed to the full. One of his main principles in teaching mathematics was to show the close connexion of every step with the needs of ordinary life. He described how geometry had begun, as its name implies, from the need to measure out the fields, after the Nile had flooded away the boundaries every year. A book on the subject had been discovered with a date some two thousand years B.C. and Euclid was only the author of a 'modern text-book'.

His plan of teaching little children to intuit numbers by the use of playing-card patterns has now become a common-place, but in those days it was a striking change from learning the multiplication table by heart. In ordinary school work he considered that the usual stumbling-block was division, owing to the two quite separate meanings of the word, and these two meanings had to be cleared up. I fancy that the maddening 'docility' of the average woman student must have broken his spirit, for later on, when he was writing to congratulate me on my first-born, he said, 'Be sure not to teach your children the stuff I talked about; teach them in the old-fashioned way; it pays better; memory, I fear, will always triumph over reason.'

A great contrast to Mr. Harding's ready acquiescence met me in the professor of classics, Mr. Platt, who required cork-screw methods to induce him to give us a lecture of any kind.

'B-but, my dear Miss Thomas,' he stammered, 'there is b-but one way to t-teach Latin. There are no d-dodges or short cuts. Latin has to be *learnt.*'

'Quite,' I readily rejoined, 'but could you point out its value when once it *is* learnt? A young pupil asked me that question once, and I was put to it to give her a ready answer.'

I believe this aspect of the matter was quite new to him. He stroked his chin in silence for a bit, and then said, 'Very well, I'll d-do my b-best.'

Unlike Mr. Allen, who had poured forth his indignation in a stream of extempore fervour, and unlike Mr. Harding with his light-hearted chat, Mr. Platt had written out his whole lecture on blue draft-paper (for I believe that in his lighter moments he was a barrister). Only one point in his brief, or rather opinion, on the teaching of classics remains in my memory, and that because of its oddity. He maintained that one great value of the study of Latin was that it acted as a corrective to Christianity. (Here we all sat up and took sharp notice.) While our established religion exhorted us to offer the other cheek to the smiter, the whole spirit of Latin literature suggested that we should smite back good and hard. The combination of the two had made England what she was. I longed to ask him *what* England was. He was too wary to elaborate the subtle satire of his statement, and I wondered afterwards whether he was even conscious of it.

I had hardly written these words when the answer to my wondering came to hand, in the shape of a letter to *The Times* which runs thus:

May I add to the unpublished fragments of verse by A. E. Housman an amusing distich, which I had from the late W. P. Ker.

A colleague and great friend of Housman's at University College, London, was the late Arthur Platt, Professor of Greek there.

Housman and Platt infused 'a certain liveliness' into the serious pages of the *Journal of Philology* by tilting at each other in jesting, but friendly, fashion.

In reference to these sparrings Housman made these two lines, which deserve not to be forgotten:

'Philology was tame and dull and flat;
God said "Let there be larks," and there was Platt!'[1]

Obviously there was no unconscious humour in Mr. Platt. I only wish we had been provocative enough to get some more of his larks.

Professor Herkomer's lecture on Art was more practical for his art-students than for any one endeavouring to teach. He gave a most amusing account of the proceedings when the selection committee for the Royal Academy were doing their selecting. He advised any one who aspired to have a picture accepted to make it long horizontally and short vertically. 'There's a great shortage of pictures of this shape,' said he, 'and we'll accept the poorest stuff, to fill the empty spaces on the walls.'

[1] From Francis Pember, All Souls, Oxford, 7 Nov. 1936.

Another year he was unable to deliver a lecture himself, but was kind enough to write a paper for us, and send one of his underlings to read it. The underling was more artistic than literary, and read so badly that the students could take no sensible notes, and I was roused from semi-somnolence by hearing the amazing statement: 'Such a course of work will enable you to reach the gaol of your ambition.'

For Art I had to fall back on my own resources. I had kept up my hobby of studying in the National Gallery, and I induced several of the students to catch my enthusiasm. Miss Worley, one of my best, essayed to give a course of lessons on Italian art in one of our schools, and even took a party of her pupils to the Gallery. How chagrined she was that it was almost impossible to get them past Frith's *Derby Day*, and that they admired the frame of a Fra Angelico far more than the picture. She and I then laughed together over Rousseau's wise remark that the greater the picture the simpler should be the frame.

Yet another variety from our College staff was afforded by the science specialist, a woman. She was quite the wisest person I have ever known—a living reproof to the foolish. 'A fine morning!' was my greeting to her one day in the cloak-room. 'I have not had time to think of the weather,' was her almost reproachful reply. She was too conscientious to say 'Yes' without due consideration.

Much to my surprise she was only too ready to give a lecture to my people, and I was grateful indeed that she would spare the time. As for myself, I knew no science. Like Arthur Sidgwick I had 'not even taught it'. So I was prepared to learn a great deal about its proper place and treatment in the schools. What was my dismay to find that instead of giving her views on such points she spent the entire time in arguing the importance of knowing one's own subject (a quite unnecessary point to labour) and the utter futility of the training of teachers. In short, she was letting off her spleen in a way that could be no possible use to the students. However, her depressing remarks aroused so much indignation in her audience that more

good than harm resulted. But I took care not to ask her help
in the succeeding years.

By the third term we had all become enthusiastic in the work
and found the time too short for the programme. Nervous
as to the reception of 'educational polity', I introduced it as a
dull subject, a necessary grind, and so on. But I managed to
clothe it as a kind of story, and as the pathetic struggle for a
decent education and better conditions for English children
was unfolded, in as dry and matter-of-fact tones as I could
achieve, the interest of the students warmed and it became
the most welcome item of the week. I was able to illustrate
the story, not only by pictures of a vast mass of children being
taught by a 'monitor', and of old-fashioned dame schools, but
also by my visit as a child to a dame school in a Cornish cottage,
and by some of Arthur's memories of similar oddities in Wales.
What interested them most was my description of one of the
very earliest (I suppose) play-centres in the East End of London.
When I was at the North London School in the eighties some
of the teachers ran such a centre in Stepney, hiring a large
room and inviting any children to come for play once or twice
a week. It was always crowded, and on one occasion a little
person aged three arrived, clad in absolutely nothing but a
piece of old shawl pinned round her. At this point in my
lecture, a student leaned forward and said, 'Do you call this
dull?'

§ 3

Meanwhile my 'home' conditions, although better than the
Kensington boarding-house, were not ideal. By a stroke of
luck an old Cambridge friend of mine, Miss Rogers, got a post
at the Baker Street High School just as I began at Bedford
College, so that we were to be working within a stone's-throw
of one another, and agreed to take rooms together. We had a
bedroom each and shared a tiny sitting-room. This was fit for
meals but nothing else, for the table was too small to work at,
in view of the vast piles of history exercise-books that Miss
Rogers brought home to correct. And we had a running

accompaniment to all our activities from the adjoining house—
a voice that kept up an obbligato of 'Ta-ra-ra-boom-de-ay'. It
sounded like a small boy, but why was he not in school? Illness
could not have kept him at home, for obviously he was in rude
health. We never solved the mystery, and he never changed
his tune. For me, owing to my previous training with the
music students, 'Ta-ra-ra-boom-de-ay' became merely blended
with the ugly furniture, but poor Miss Rogers was driven to her
bedroom.

Our meals still give me a shiver in retrospect, for they were
nearly always cold mutton. The little joint was hot on Sunday,
and then lasted through the week. Once we asked to have it
warmed up, but the charge for gravy was so excessive that we
couldn't or wouldn't afford a repetition. I have great sympathy
with Rhodes, who is said to have attributed his success in life
to cold mutton. He suffered so much from it as a child that he
determined to make himself rich enough never to have to eat
it again. To us, life-savers came occasionally from our homes
in the west—Devon and Cornwall—in the blessed shape of
eggs, butter, cream, jam, fruits, buns, and pasties. Among
these a bottle of pickles from Cornwall stands out pre-eminent,
for it enabled us to swallow more mouthfuls of that cold
mutton. One day some eggs arrived in a smashed condition,
and we asked to have them made into a custard. It was a
splendid affair, and we ate in rapture, but checked our appetites so as to keep half for the next day. What was our chagrin
to learn from the dastard lips of our landlady that she had 'put
it away'. We knew the dreadful significance of this phrase,
and although Miss Rogers let loose a good rush of winged
words, we both knew that they could not recall our custard,
which had gone into the great beyond.

One day Miss Rogers came in with the exciting news that
a grand building had been opened quite near, called the Ladies'
Residential Chambers. We hurried off to see it and make
inquiries, full of rosy visions of being free of landladies for
ever, and able to eat our rice-pudding under our own fig-tree.
We found a dignified Lady Superintendent, who informed us

that every applicant must have references and must agree to certain regulations, of which the chief seemed to be that no nail must be driven into the walls. There was a flat available on the top floor, containing two rooms and a third little place, half kitchen, half scullery. One bathroom, charged extra, had to serve all the flats on one floor. There were six stories and no lift. Well, it seemed to us the promised land, and we spent all our spare time figuring out the cost. The rent was high and we had no furniture, but we reckoned that in the long run we should spend less than in our lodgings, and get infinitely more comfort. And I reflected that any furniture I bought would come in useful when I was married. How we enjoyed prowling round the little back streets in search of bargains—chairs, a gaunt table 'salvaged' from a fire, and a rickety writing-desk that Mary Wood called the 'demon bureau' on account of its hideous appearance. It deserved the name from its many drawers, into which I put things and lost them, often shaking the whole concern into its component parts in frantic efforts to find them. One looking-glass we bought was so vile that it discouraged vanity. Nothing will destroy this bit of our furniture, and it hangs in my kitchen to-day, the hero of a hundred moves. Some of my brother Charles's pictures enlivened my walls, and Dym sent me a pound to spend on curtains. Meals gave us no trouble, for a good dinner was served in the common dining-room, lunch was either a picnic affair at home or else taken at a tea-shop, and our gas-ring was enough for breakfast requirements. This we used to eat together in the 'kitchen'. We shared the labour thus: Miss Rogers 'laid' the eggs overnight, and I cooked them in the morning. If we both chanced to be in at lunch time we unbent over a game of halma. There was no time or brain-vitality for chess, but just enough for halma. We became so adept at this foolish game that the one who had first move was sure to win.

The evening dinner was always a pleasant interlude, for we met a variety of interesting women, all of them at work of some kind—artists, authors, political workers, and so on. There was one artist with whom I became specially friendly

owing to our common interest in early Italian art. She persuaded me to make copies of details from the pictures in the
National Gallery, since it would teach me more than any
amount of reading about the painters. She thought Ruskin
was all very well, but you could have too much of him. I
have never been grateful enough to her for these talks at
dinner. Once or twice a week I used to go to the Gallery and
make little sketches as I stood, and soon came to know the
various schools, the painters' styles, and the individual pictures.
I used to take my efforts down to dinner to show Miss Harwood, and she would criticize splendidly, sometimes praising
and sometimes saying, 'No. That won't do. You can do much
better than that.' I think she suffered more than most people
from ugly sights and stupid companions; she told me how
some visitor would remark on leaving that she had had a
pleasant time, 'Little thinking,' added Miss Harwood, 'that
I was exhausted; such people are blood-suckers.' I am not so
sensitive myself, but often enough feel that people take more
out of one than they give.

Sitting next me at dinner one evening was an influential
member of the staff of the Baker Street High School, and as
she chatted she said:

'I hear that you share a flat with our Miss Rogers. . . . I
wonder whether you could induce her to be a little less conscientious?'

'I've tried often enough,' I said, laughing, 'to persuade her
that the girls never dream of reading all the long red-ink com-
ments that she makes on their exercise-books. But surely there
has been no actual complaint about it?'

'Oh, no. But the other day I overheard a group of children
in the cloakroom. "What's the next lesson?" asked one.
"Baiting Rogy," was the reply. By some discreet detective
work I discovered that these little demons manage to spend
a large part of the lesson in arguing about the marks: "Please
may I have a mark for this?" or more effective still, "Please
you have given me a mark too much." And although poor
Miss Rogers gets flustered and annoyed at the waste of time,

she attends to each plea as though she were a High Court Judge. No wonder they enjoy it!'

I hadn't the heart to pass this on to Miss Rogers, but I told it (properly disguised) to my students, as a warning of what an enlargement of the conscience might produce. Providence had endowed this friend of mine, I told them, with a mind full of splendid stuff, 'instead of which' she spent her evenings in paltry corrections, when she might have gone to a theatre or been for a country walk, and come next morning all fresh and jolly to give a rousing review of the Civil War, or what not, that would correct their historical faults at a blow; and what mattered spelling faults? Such trifles any sensible teacher ought to put right politely as she goes.

I used to tempt Miss Rogers to a theatre as often as I could, and several times we went to the Court Theatre in grand style, for a cousin of hers owned it and used to send us tickets for the stalls. We could stay out till any hour, for although the main door was locked at eleven, each tenant had a latch-key. Miss Rogers had a nasty trick of asking me suddenly, at some poignant moment of the play, 'Did you remember to bring the key?' I determined to cure her of this by a bit of strategy; pretending to hunt through all my pockets in desperate anxiety, I looked at her in dismay, and wondered where on earth we could go for the night. When she had suffered enough I told her that I should repeat this performance every time she so much as mentioned the key in future.

What with our work and our recreations we led a happy life together, but I felt it rather unfair that I should have so many more of life's good things than she had. For by this time Arthur had been 'called' and had taken the plunge of coming to London to start his legal career. So once a week at least we used to meet and go for a long country walk or prowl about the unfrequented historical bits of the City or visit some picture gallery; and on Sunday we went to the morning service at the Temple, to enjoy good music and an extremely learned sermon. All the little contretemps of the week were blown away during these outings.

Epping Forest was one of our favourite haunts, and with some difficulty we discovered the old cottage, Little Monkhams, in which I had been born. It stood among the trees, within a few hundred yards of the railway near Buckhurst Hill Station, where my father used to start for the City every morning. It is still standing as I write to-day, but is not long for this world, for new houses of the 'Monkhams Estate', with all modern conveniences, are creeping up to it.

Arthur had taken temporary lodgings in Great Coram Street, sinister in sound and appearance. I do not care to let my fancy roam over his diet during this period. He told me that an aggressively successful barrister said to him one day, 'Ah, Hughes, what do you do, ah, about lunch?' 'Oh, that's simple enough,' replied Arthur, 'if I have any money I have lunch, and if not I don't.'

His first case in Court was an excitement for both of us. I had a telegram with the single word 'Won', and on the following evening went with him and his solicitor to the pantomime. The choice of entertainment lay with the solicitor who bought the seats, and we managed to conceal our boredom through the whole show—transformation scene, clown-tricks, and everything.

Soon after this he managed to get quarters in Gray's Inn, some delightful old oak-panelled rooms in Field Court, in a building subsequently pulled down. Indeed it was in a shaky condition even then. But how lovely the flavour of the rooms and how easily they were comfortably furnished with two deep basket chairs, a second-hand table, and two of Charles's pictures on the walls. And the big windows looked out on Gray's Inn Gardens, with the cawing of rooks and memories of Bacon. Arthur was 'done for' by his laundress, Mrs. Keyes, one of the most lovable women I have ever met. Rosy-cheeked, of uncertain age, invariably bonneted, she appeared to rejoice in her work, which was mostly confined to cooking breakfast on a small gas-stove, and tidying up generally. I asked Arthur why she was called a 'laundress', and he said that the usually accepted theory was that laundresses were so called because they never washed anything. What she enjoyed most was the arrival of visitors. And of these there was no lack. The brothers of the family, 'the boys' as I always called them, were the most frequent visitors. The parson brother, Llewelyn, used to like an excuse to run up to town to see that the bishops were doing their duty at some Assembly or other. The doctor brother, Alfred, was now professor of anatomy at Cardiff, and very well off, and couldn't keep away from London for long. My own brothers, Tom and Dym, were equally bitten with the love of the old town, and could always be sure of a hearty welcome and a shake-down in the ample rooms in Field Court. Of course no casual visitor ever invaded Arthur's sacred room in the Temple, complete with law-books and clerk.

In the spring of '93 the best visitor of all arrived. My sailor brother Barnholt had three weeks' leave. This he parcelled out between us. Dym met him at Plymouth and kept him for the first week, then he went to Tom in Yorkshire for the second week, and the last week he spent in Gray's Inn. Tom and Dym stole a week-end from their work to run up to town, anxious to have every possible moment with their favourite brother. I used to go over to tea, to 'pour out' for them all, and enjoy the endless talk, and be chaffed and teased as in the old days at home in Canonbury. Two or three times Barnholt ventured to the Ladies' Residential Chambers, to see that I was all right. He was a bit overawed by Miss Rogers, who was extremely large, and he insisted on giving her what she called the brevet title of *Mrs.* Rogers. She took the liveliest interest in all the boys, and especially in Arthur. As for herself, she had a most charming mother who used to come to see us now and again, but of love-story she had none. She told me that at the age of sixteen she looked in her mirror and said, 'You are very plain; make up your mind once for all that no one will ever want to marry you.' There seemed to me more heroism and pathos in this than in lots of novels, for instead of being soured by her unattractive appearance she was full of wit and humour and warm-heartedness. She was fond of what she called the 'three-volume' story of the Devon maiden: 'the first time she married was because she was young and silly-like; the second time she married it was for cows and sich; but the third time she married it was for pure, pure *lov*.'

During the few hours that Barnholt spent in Gray's Inn when Arthur and the others were not there, he was fully entertained by Mrs. Keyes. She dusted the room over and over again while he regaled her with yarns of dreadful storms 'round the Horn' in a sailing vessel, with the sailors on their knees in despair. And she had quite as harrowing disclosures to make of horrors in Gray's Inn.

'Down below 'ere, Sir, in these 'ere very buildings, there's corpses.'

She had been during one spell of her lurid career a kitchen-hand in a London restaurant, and had seen things.

'Don't you never eat in no restaurant, Sir. Me and Keyes could tell you things . . . what they does to make the vegetables green! and the thick soup! Ah!'

The dear soul broke down with genuine grief when the news came, some two months later, of Barnholt's death in South America.

III

America Calling

THE long vacation of '93 was close at hand, and Cornwall in my mind's eye, when I had a surprise. I had been selected to represent Bedford College at Chicago. The 'World's Fair' was being held there, a huge exhibition of everything, outshining our London 'Fisheries', Naval Exhibition, and such-like. In connexion with it, as a kind of serious sideshow, was a big Educational Conference. My duties were to be simple, merely to attend any meetings that seemed useful, to read at one of them a paper by Mrs. Bryant, and to write a report when I returned. Expenses were to be paid, and there was nothing to prevent my going. My natural advisers, Arthur, Dym, and Tony, were all for my seizing such a chance. They had all travelled abroad and knew the value of seeing strange places, and I had seen nothing more foreign than Wales and Cornwall; and as for a sea voyage, the only steamboat I had experienced was a penny paddle-boat on the Thames.

The eight of us who had been chosen from various schools and colleges met at a house in Gower Street, to be introduced to each other and to receive final instructions and books of tickets from Mrs. Henry Fawcett. For travel on board ship she told us that the most useful thing was a hold-all, about a foot and a half square, made of brown holland, and endowed with pockets of different sizes, to contain slippers, brush and comb, handkerchiefs, and so on. It could be rolled up with a strap, and made to carry odds and ends. With this and a cabin-trunk we should be complete. I bought the cabin-trunk with comparative ease, but spent several feverish hours of the short time left in concocting, with the help of Miss Rogers, this confounded hold-all. It caused Arthur much amusement, but beyond this it had no advantages. Seldom was anything in its right pocket, no article was really held and the whole contraption (intended to be hung by tapes in the cabin) was never within reach when wanted.

Arthur arranged a pleasant treat for the evening before I was to start, a concert at the Albert Hall, to hear Patti (her 'positively last appearance'). London was gay with flags and flowers and illuminations, to celebrate the royal wedding, and the initials G and M were everywhere. All I remember of the concert was the glorious voice of Patti, and the thrill that ran through the audience at her encore when the first notes of 'Home Sweet Home' reached us. I can still hear the long-drawn beauty of the word 'home' as she filled the vast hall with it, and the thunder of applause when the song closed.

The following evening Arthur came to put me and my belongings on a cab and see me off by the night train for Liverpool. 'I've put in my pocket,' said he, 'a small flask of brandy for you to put in that hold-all, because you never know.' Trying to be funny at Euston I asked an official which was the platform for New York. 'Number 15. Change at Liverpool' was the reply immediately snapped out at me. Arthur was full of anxieties and final instructions, and it was not until the train was gathering speed that I realized that he had forgotten to give me his flask. On arrival at Liverpool I fell in with the three educational delegates who were to travel with me. No city is at its best at six o'clock in the morning, and after a prowl round the streets until it was possible to get an hotel breakfast, we felt that we had sucked the pleasures of Liverpool dry, and were glad to go aboard.

Our boat was the *Adriatic*, never one of the latest type of ocean greyhound, I imagine, and now nearing its age for retirement. But to me it seemed both spacious and amusing. We were travelling second class and had a cabin between the four of us, and much happy time was consumed in arranging our luggage and exploring the vessel. Why this awkward wooden bar at the entrance to our cabin I asked, why little holders for the glasses, how do I get up into my berth, do we all wash out of this basin? As soon as we started all other interests were sunk in the delight of watching the sea, but

towards late afternoon I began to be what Jane Austen calls
'a little disordered', climbed up to my top berth, and didn't
feel like climbing down again.

That was the first day. We were told that the voyage
would take ten days, but they seemed like a hundred. I envied
my companions who were able to get up, have meals, go on
deck, and apparently enjoy themselves, and I sucked what
amusement I could from watching their oddities. One slept
extremely well and snored unfailingly. Another was of a
literary turn and begged us not to gaze on her Dianic form
while she washed. The third seemed to have an obsession
about her belongings and was always rearranging her luggage.
When they had gone up on deck I had the cabin to myself for
the bulk of the day. It was then that I suffered from claustro-
phobia, in addition to my nausea. The top of our cabin was
only about a foot above my head—quite bearable at night,
but incredibly oppressive all day long. After a struggle down
for a wash, up again I would climb, and get some distraction
from 'noises without'. These consisted chiefly of the sounds
of people hurrying to and fro, and I guessed that we must be
between the dining-room and the kitchen, for amid the medley
of shouting, snatches of popular songs, and the clash of wash-
ing-up, I discerned orders for food: 'Irish stew for a lady' (was
this a small portion?) 'Dry 'ash four times.' I tried to picture
what dry 'ash could possibly be, but am ignorant to this day;
Arthur saw it on a restaurant menu some months later, and
ordered it so that he might tell me, but said that he would rather
not refer to the subject again. At night the sound of scrubbing
predominated, except during one period of the voyage when
the fog-horn drowned all music but its own. I rather liked
this, for it suggested the possibility of a collision when the
roof of the cabin might be broken. The stewardess was a
cheerful body who said 'Yus' to everything, and I suppose she
must have brought me something to swallow now and again.
She assured me that I should be well by Wednesday, because
people always were. Wednesday came and went, and I still lay
there thinking of the riddle of my childhood that compared

the *Adriatic* to a dry attic. I thought too of the rich man's reply to his steward's 'What can I fetch you, Sir?'—'Fetch me an island.' I could raise a laugh over this, for I remembered from geography lessons that the good old Atlantic was five miles deep.

One afternoon as I lay there, going over such silly ideas and shutting my eyes against that terrible ceiling, I felt the unmistakable touch of a man's hand, laid, large and gentle, on mine. Turning my head I opened my eyes on a tall and kindly looking man in uniform.

'Who are you?' I asked, smiling with pleasure at any break to my thoughts.

'I'm the ship's doctor,' said he, 'and you must try to come up on deck, or you will be really ill.'

Cheered by his mere manner I struggled into some clothes and found some one to help me along the passages and up on to the deck again. How lovely was the fresh air and the sight of the sea, and the sound of the talk of the others. They welcomed me heartily, one wrapped a rug round me and another brought me a tot of brandy, and I knew then for the first time the magic effect of this godsend of a restorative. Time didn't hang so heavily now, but I think that Columbus himself was not more pleased at a sight of America than I to have Long Island pointed out to me, to see fireworks ashore and the varied lights of the shipping that we were passing. Sickness left me and I even made my way into the dining-room and ordered something to eat.

We docked early in the morning, and my first contact with America was the big customs-shed of New York. The officials were tall and leisurely, always sucking something and completely indifferent to any one's concerns. It gave me an absurd shock to hear them talking English quite easily, and me having come all that way! The four of us who had shared a cabin kept together for mutual protection, and ventured forth into the streets. They seemed much like those at home, only far noisier. We tried a little restaurant for lunch, and greatly amused the people by our ignorance of the strange coinage.

Refreshed, we began to look about, and presently one of us discovered through some advertisement that it was possible to go to Washington by train. We knew that Washington was the capital, but it seemed a long way off, and we had no notion that trains were common enough in America for people to go about casually as we did in England.

'But what about Chicago?' I demurred. 'We have to get there somehow, and Cook's man has told us how to.'

'Oh, but there's sure to be some kind of railway-line to get there from Washington,' argued the bolder spirit, 'and we may never in our lives have the chance to see Washington if we don't now. Oh do let's.'

So we all went to the station, after learning to our amusement that we must never ask for the 'station' (a very different place), but for the 'depot'. Here we found ourselves among a large number of passengers, just like one sees at Liverpool Street Station on any Saturday afternoon. Only in New York there was no agitated speculation as to which platform or what hour. Every one was seated comfortably in an airy waiting-room until the summons came for the train. 'Why can't we go on the platform,' I wondered. I soon saw the reason. There was no platform. We had to step up into the train from the line, or 'track' as they called it. Here were fresh surprises for us. Instead of the stuffy little upholstered compartments on our English railways (where people never agree as to how much fresh air may be let in) there were spacious, long, open carriages, where we could move about in comfort, change our seats so as to get different points of view, arrange our belongings, and make frequent excursions to the end of the car where iced water was provided free! We had hardly started when white-coated boys came along, proclaiming for sale all sorts of little luxuries—magazines, fans, tempting fruit, candy. . . . When I exclaimed that it seemed to me a kind of fairyland, one of our party argued that it was all very well for the Americans to have all these modern improvements, but it was the English who had started railways, and had to work off the old stock. I was obliged to concede this point, but felt more sympathy with her next remark about the views from the windows, which compared unfavourably enough with our English country-side: she said that her respect for the Pilgrim Fathers was much increased, for they must have been extremely earnest about their religion to leave England for America. I wished we could have seen more of Philadelphia than we managed to spy from the railway, for Penn had always been one of my heroes.

However, Washington made up for all and exceeded my best expectations. In mid-July this lovely city was hotter than anything I had ever experienced, but was a dream of delight. White and green were the prevailing tones, from beautiful houses and huge trees. Spacious streets were being continually watered with great splashing hoses that made our little lumbering water-carts seem funny in comparison. There were few people about at that time of year, and our hotel was nearly empty, and hardly any attendants to be seen. After consulting with one another we rang for the chambermaid, and a negro appeared! But he was quite efficient for all we wanted. My chief need was a bath, and I never enjoyed one so much before or since. Then a real bed to lie down in. My first night in America will never fade from my memory.

We were up early the next morning to make the most of the few hours before we were to start for Chicago. The Capitol astounded us; we had no idea that the Americans knew how to build anything so large and impressive. But we were far more fascinated by the White House, a homely looking villa so near the roadway that we felt inclined to tap on the window and ask how they were getting on.

How silent and dignified the city seemed on that Sunday afternoon as we made our way to the depot to get our train for Chicago. But here we came upon a new phase of American life. The depot was all a-bustle with negroes starting on excursions. Believe me, I had always pictured negroes, if not naked, attired in the minimum, or in white garments of some slight kind. Here they were out-doing our 'Ampstead 'Arries and 'Arriets in the colour and extravagant splendour of their holiday clothes. I had a chat with a woman who was carrying a real live black baby in a snow-white dress. She was pleased at my admiring the little fellow, and let me hold him a bit. I was sorry to leave Washington.

Our first point of excitement on the journey was Harper's Ferry. This romantic spot actually existed, and there we were, passing through it quite casually. Our enthusiasm amused our fellow passengers, some of whom appeared to know less about John Brown than we did. I was struck with the extreme readiness of these people to talk to us and start a temporary friendship. My own family had always been inclined to chat with a traveller at any time, but our chattiness was cool reserve compared to that of Americans. At first I was a little on the defensive, but soon began to enjoy and appreciate this general friendliness. After all it's the best way to 'see' a country, and get various opinions and meet new people; and there was the ever-blessed link of a common language. A common language, yes, but every one spotted us as English. 'How do you know I'm English?' I asked a pleasant sea-captain who begged to join us at our tea in the 'parlour car', and entertained us with yarns from a world-wide experience. His reply was immediate: 'By your way of talking and by your bright complexion.' It was news to me that I had either.

When dusk fell our negro porter came to make up our couches for the night. Now I had not been anything but hot since leaving New York, and I besought him not to pile on the rugs. 'You're hot now,' said he, 'but wait till we are going over the Alleghanies, and see if you don't pull them round you.' I lay down and enjoyed the quiet evening effect as the sun was setting over the hills, and then there came over me that odd feeling (that has always attacked me at intervals) of being alone in the world, and I began to wonder what on earth I was doing careering over a strange continent. Not for long; the negro was right; the night grew cold, and rolling myself up in my rugs I fell happily asleep.

In the morning we managed to have a sketchy kind of wash in the train. It was badly needed, for the soot on a railway journey in America was like nothing we get in England. Great lumps of soot nestled into our clothes. Our captain explained it as due to the softness of the coal, so nothing could be done about it. We were indeed sorry to say good-bye to this Captain Riley, who was going on, while we had to change for Chicago. We talked eagerly of the meal we intended to have at the junction, picturing a kind of Bristol refreshment room, for the tea in the 'parlour car' had not been very sustaining, and it was now eight o'clock in the morning. But Cincinnati Junction turned out to be no more than a wooden track, with a small shed on it. This shed was evidently a refreshment-room, but all that was left to eat consisted of two buns on a glass dish. 'How much are these buns?' said I to the woman presiding over them. Staring at me she exclaimed in rich nasal twang, 'How funny you do talk!' When I laughed and said that we had come from an outlandish place called England, she said we could have the buns for nothing (although she called them by some other word which I forget). These didn't go far to stay the hunger of the four of us, and as we were wondering rather dismally where and when our next meal would be, in came the Chicago express. We had hardly taken our seats when a white-robed waiter stalked along the train, proclaiming in each car the joyful news: 'Breakfast is served in the rear car.' Course after course was placed before us, including fruit, porridge and cream, omelettes, fish, and cutlets. We enjoyed as much as the swaying of the train allowed us to convey to our mouths, and with much laughter we agreed that the waiter deserved a good tip, although the price of the breakfast itself was a bit staggering. I said that I had plenty of change and would see to the tip. A shilling seemed to me handsome enough, and I left on the table what I took to be a shilling, but I noticed as we were leaving the car that the waiter looked anything but pleased, and it was not till several hours later that I realized the value of the nickel I had so generously given him.

We felt that another meal in that train was beyond our means, and arrived at Chicago at about 6.30 in the evening, very tired, dirty, and hungry. Different places for boarding had been assigned to us, so our foursome party was split up.

Two of us were to be lodged at the University, and looked forward with confidence to an immediate and pleasant reception. We pictured the University as a dignified cluster of colleges in some prominent part of the town, as well known to the inhabitants as King's is to Cambridge people. Having been warned that cabmen were apt to be extortionate we thought to economize by taking the elevated railway, but there was no ready response when we asked for tickets to take us as near the University as possible. Each person consulted recommended a different station to aim at. So we tried one after another along the line, looking out in vain for anything that suggested a university. Back and forth we went, and it was now getting dark. One fellow traveller strongly recommended the Exhibition station, and although anything more unlike a university than an exhibition it was hard to imagine, we determined to get out and give the idea a trial. We started off walking along several unmade roads deep in dust, getting no nearer anywhere promising. I was wearing the slippers into which I had changed for the railway journey, and they were hardly the thing for a suburban walk in Chicago in the dark. Ploughing through one road I left a shoe stuck in the soil, and as I retrieved it I thought of Tadpole's similar accident and laughed. 'There's nothing to laugh at,' said my companion. 'We don't want to be out here all night, and there's not even a cab to be had in this region.' Just then I spied a kind of open café, with lights and people moving about. We went in and told them our plight. They were very kind and brought out a map of Chicago. Accustomed to the complexity of London, with its muddle but at least a few main streets, I was defeated by this chess-board of straight roads crossing one another at right angles and all apparently of equal importance, and numbered like convicts. But those in the know read it quite easily, and our good Samaritans soon found that the University was indeed close to the Exhibition. So we must have been circling round it all the time.

What with the soot of the railway and the dust of the streets we felt quite unfit for a dignified arrival at the University. We needn't have worried; there was a warm welcome for us from those who had already arrived and were getting anxious about us; there was a copious supper covered by netting to keep the flies off; various kinds of baths and bed-rooms; and all troubles were soon drowned in sound sleep. Next morning I was quickly at my window to see my surroundings by daylight. When I saw the extremely new buildings and the wooden planks laid on the ground for people to walk from one to another, I began to see that the whole thing was still 'in the making', and to wonder no longer that the bulk of the people of Chicago had not yet heard of their university. After all, I reflected, even Oxford itself must have been new once, or at least parts of it now and then, like Keble; and I tried to picture what Chicago University would be like in a few thousand years.

I went down to breakfast and found the supper-room of the night before a noisy scramble of catch-as-catch-can. But there was plenty to eat and general camaraderie among the strangers from all quarters who were boarded in the University—some fifty in number. The Educational Congress was being held in a large building in another part of the town, and a party of us started off all business-like with note-books. I ran back to fetch something from my room and was shocked to find my bed being made by a negro. It was not that he was a negro, but that a man should be doing such a domestic and intimate job . . . a job that I used to do for my brothers, but the other way about seemed all wrong. When I breathed my discomfiture to the others they laughed and told me I should soon get used to it. But I never did, and kept well away when this menial task was due.

Our short daily journey was on the Illinois Central overhead railway. The little stations and carriages were all primitive and ramshackly; there were no doors at all to the compartments; we were kept in by a long iron bar which was worked by the guard: he would pull it back at each station for a few moments, for people to get in or out, and they had to nip about quickly for fear of being caught by the bar in transit. In principle it was like our modern sliding doors on the Tube, but how different in practice!

Any one who has ever looked in at an Educational Conference needs no description of it. The same uplifting speeches are delivered at them all, no doubt the same that bored the Athenians and drove the Romans to the Baths. Of the many that we endured at Chicago I have memories of only two: a rousing, straight-from-the-shoulder, human address from Commissioner Harris; and the curious contrast of a paper read by the Russian Prince Sergius, whose deliberate style and old-world polish enchanted me. Most of the American speakers took themselves more seriously than English people do, and were correspondingly more wearisome. The real value of such conferences lies in the discussions in corridors and side-rooms, at lunches and teas, when teachers will confess to strangers what they really do do, where they have despaired, and where succeeded a bit. They recommend books to one another and pore together over the publishers' stalls. In Chicago these were good, and I made many casual friends while discussing and buying. Teachers had come from great distances and were obviously enjoying a good time, perhaps their best holiday for many years. I think Chaucer would find good scope to-day for more tales among these modern pilgrims, and instead of the old slogan 'St. Thomas is the best doctor' we might have a new one—'An Educational Conference is the best doctor' —for it gives teachers a change physically and mentally, if it is only to see the absurdity of their own solemnity.

Those few of us who were English graduates were referred to as *alumnae*, and were amused to find ourselves lionized and invited hither and thither. I actually spent a week-end at the home of a wealthy Chicago merchant, who had a 'place' on the lake-side. This was my one and only chance to be for longer than an hour or two inside a real American home, and it was quite unlike what I expected. The house was large and 'well appointed' in every way, but there was total lack of domestic service, even of 'coloured help'. Meals were on a big scale, but the mother cooked, and we all fetched what we wanted, cleared away, washed up, and so on, with great fun. This struck me as a far more satisfactory arrangement than one finds in some English households, where there is more service than things served. My chief pleasure was in their only child, a little girl of four who did her best to get in the way of everybody and make me romp with her on the grand staircase.

One other example of American hospitality stands out in my memory. A Mrs. Catsinger, of Austin, invited a few of us one afternoon to meet her husband and children and some American *alumnae*. We didn't go into the house, but were entertained in a large garden, where quite a poetical meal was served as we 'sat around'. A full-sized English butler with his satellites brought salads and ices and most unusual little cakes of a dainty kind, as well as varied drinks. Conversation was at a high level, but not heavy or self-conscious; as an intellectual treat it was the best I had in Chicago.

As an extreme contrast to this I recall a visit to what was called a Chatauqua meeting, a kind of blend of education and religion. To these people the teaching of the young seemed to be too solemn and important to talk about calmly, and I was obliged to come away quite hurriedly.

Our two chief amusements, when the rigours of the conference were over for the day, were the Exhibition and shopping. To examine the shop-windows of a strange town is an unfailing source of recreation to a Londoner. I was puzzled by these in Chicago. Drapery was easy to find, but there appeared to be no simple bakers or grocers or chemists. I wanted some biscuits, and tried to describe them to a kindly shopkeeper. It is really harder to describe a biscuit than you would think. 'Oh,' he exclaimed at last, 'what you want is crackers.' 'No, no,' I protested, picturing the bon-bons of Christmas time. But he was right, and I learnt another American word. We should have spent more time in prowling about the city and watching people at work, if the streets had not been so filthy with spitting. No English person would believe how bad it was, requiring us to pick every step we took on the pavements in even the best streets. And in the trams it was far worse, because there was less accommodation for the disgusting habit. So we generally gravitated to the World's Fair, which was kept, by some unknown means, beautifully clean, in spite of the crowds of people. But cleanliness isn't everything, and I missed the tang of Chicago's reality. Just like conferences, all exhibitions and fairs are very much alike— grand white temporary palaces, artificial lake, lit by fairy lights, Javan and Indian villages (one native village was rather too realistic with its war-cries), Saratoga gold-mine, glass-blowing, gun-making, and a big Transportation building. The midway Plaisance afforded endless side-shows (including 'a peep at your future home' and a Congress of Beauty). Restaurants at every corner were convenient and tempting but ruinously expensive. A phonograph band produced a more hideous noise than any I had previously known. On the whole I preferred the dirty streets, but was certainly shocked at the river of Chicago, in which I think a spoon would easily have stood up.

So far as we could discover there was no important 'sight' in Chicago that visitors were supposed to 'do'. The only special thing that we had associated with the town was the pork factory, but we had been warned not on any account to visit the stock-yard, because the killing of the pigs was an insufferable sight. Of course we had heard that the organization was so complete that the pig walked in at one end and came out at the other in the form of sausages. Two of our party felt that such marvellous management must be well worth seeing, and really *ought* to be investigated, if Chicago was to be thoroughly visited. So they went to the office and explained to the man in charge that they wished to see something of the processes, but to avoid the actual scene of the killing. 'Sure,' said he, scenting no doubt that he had some elegant hypersensitive English ladies to deal with, and immediately he ushered them straight into the slaughter-house, where some thousand pigs were being dispatched. They rushed away and were really ill for a few hours. I had a sneaking sympathy with that man.

As soon as the conference was over our party was expected to return to England. Two of us, however, felt inclined to see some more of the continent, now we had come so far. We both had friends in Canada who had invited us to pay them a visit, and it was simply flying in the face of Providence not to go. My friend started off at once for Winnipeg, but I was only going as far as Toronto and was able to stay with the rest of our party a little longer. Our route was planned to give us a short stay at the Niagara Falls. I think we were all sorry to say good-bye to Chicago, where we had begun to feel at home, and started off on our night journey quite reluctantly. Early in the morning our train was halted to give the passengers a view of the Falls. This seemed to me extremely funny. In England one looked upon a train's business as serious—speed —getting there—that was the main consideration; the idea of stopping to look at a beauty spot was merely frivolous. Nor on reflection did I think it good policy if Americans wanted mere passers-by to see the Falls. From the train they were as disappointing as a first glimpse of Stonehenge seems to any one going by in a car. One has to come close to these monsters before one can feel the terrifying effect they must have had on the worshippers of the sun-god. And so with Niagara; it was only after we had been for an hour or two in an hotel over-looking the Falls and within sound of their roar that their grandeur seized us. While we were strolling round, getting various points of view and looking down into the whirlpool in which Captain Webb lost his life, we discovered that it was possible (for the sum of two dollars) to go right under one of the Falls. Why boggle at two dollars, we thought, for such a glory?

Accordingly the three of us went into a little wooden cabin, stripped off all our clothes and got into mackintoshes provided for us. Then we went into a rather crazy-looking lift and were lowered to the base of the Fall. Here we stepped out and fol-lowed our guide. He led us over a stony way and soon we were right under the great cataract of water. The noise was now deafening. Although well accustomed to jumping from boulder to boulder on the Cornish shore, I found these slippery rocks far worse. We were not roped, and in the semi-darkness I was aware that the least mistake of a step would send one down into the ugly backwash of the river swirling round us. I lost my nerve and yelled to the guide to take us back, but the noise was so great that I might as well have yelled to the moon. Fortunately the others had not heard me either, and were sturdily following me. In fact there was no possible means of turning safely however much we had wanted to. So, facing up to the idea that any moment might be my last, I fixed my gaze on the guide's broad back and trod forward. What a relief it was to come out from the gloom and roar, and to be able to take hold of something wooden. There is something human and comforting in the touch of wood. Is this a relic of our simian past? On looking back on that expedition, however, I think that our next bit of walk was quite as crazy an undertaking as the struggle over the wet rocks. A series of planks was placed over the foot of the Fall, and provided with a hand-rail, and along this 'bridge' we made our way amid the foam back again to our lift. There was no room for thoughts of danger, for we were quite overcome with the beauty of the scene. We looked right up at the mass of falling water dazzling white in the sunshine, with an undertone of emerald. No view from the top could ever have come near it. When the hotel clerks and visitors heard where we had been they declared that nothing would induce them to go down. We felt quite distinguished, especially as we had been given certificates to show beyond doubt that we had actually gone under the Fall.

On the next day I parted from my original cabin companions—they were for New York and England, and I took ship for Toronto, where I was to be met by my Canadian host and hostess.

IV

I Find Robinson Crusoe

§ 1

CANADA was easy. As I cruised across the lake to Toronto I felt almost like going home. I knew all about Canada. Not only *Ungava*, but *Hiawatha* and all Red Indian romances and legends and *The Last of the Mohicans*. . . . I had given all of them a Canadian setting. Then there was Wolfe, and I knew that everything was safely English.

The people I was to meet were complete strangers to me, introduced by the member of Bedford College Council who had 'supported' me. My host, Mr. Kyle, was her cousin, and I concluded that he would be of the same wealthy and influential type. In his letter giving me instructions where to meet him he said that he lived in a small village on the shores of Lake Ontario. Its name, Oakville, had an unpleasingly hybrid sound, but what did that matter? I pictured a village on the lines of a hundred English ones . . . old church, old inn, thatched cottages, village green with an old oak-tree and a pump. These people, oddly enough, actually lived in the inn . . . probably with low ceilings, old rafters, uneven floors. Again the name was a bit disconcerting—the International Hotel—rather pretentious for a village, I thought, but many inns had absurd names. The idea of being near the lake was a great attraction, for my loveliest thoughts of Canada had always been connected with the Canadian boat song, a dreamy thing we used to sing at school.

My mind was a confused medley of such expectations when I was met on the quay at Toronto by Mr. and Mrs. Kyle, and shipped off immediately on another steamer for Oakville. I was at once disabused of the idea of 'wealth and influence' in my new friends. Mr. Kyle was very tall and thin, dressed in homely 'slacks' and a hat with an immense brim. His sunburn was of the kind that suggests continual open-air life. His speech was drawling and punctuated with spitting, and his tobacco of such a nature that I kept as much to windward of him as I could without appearing to. At all points he struck me as *real*, and I took an immediate liking to him. His wife was a curious contrast, giving an air of unreality to all she said and did. Both her speech and clothes sat uncomfortably on her. It wasn't long before I discovered the reason: while he was a thoroughbred Englishman, she was a Canadian; while he had adopted Canadian life whole-heartedly and seemed to care not a snap for England, she was for ever striving to be the complete English lady.

They were both undisguisedly relieved at my appearance and manner. Almost at once they confessed that they had dreaded my visit, imagining an English girl not only learned, but full of 'frills'—a word they used to describe English fastidiousness and standoffishness. Our short run on the steamer convinced Mr. Kyle that he could be himself, and Mrs. Kyle that she need not strain so much.

We arrived at a formal little new landing-stage, and were immediately in the 'village', which was quite unlike any English one I had ever seen. The 'cottages' consisted of neat wooden shanties laid out along neat roads in square formation, as though a future Chicago had been envisaged. There were pretty gardens, but so neat, so unlike the glorious medley of flowers sprawling about the approaches to our cottages. The International Hotel was a tall, ugly, new building, but happily free from any attempt at architectural ornament. Quietly shedding my disappointment I embraced the idea that I was seeing something new and strange—an American city in its birth throes. So when Mr. Kyle asked me what I would like to see or do, I said, 'Let me potter about with you and just look'.

His first suggestion was that we should go for a row, as he had some business at a mill. The combination of a row and a mill —nothing could better fit my fancy. And I was delighted to find that he headed, not towards the tame-looking lake, but to a creek, wide and deep, of irregular course, with richly wooded banks and with water-lilies in it. Moored to the bank was the family boat, into which we all got. The Kyles had one son, aged about ten, their only child, born to them after twenty years of married life, about whom naturally there was much maternal anxiety; where exactly he was, how clothed, and what eating, absorbed most of his mother's mental life; but he was quite hearty, pert, and could spit almost as well as his father. Well, the boat was capacious enough to hold us all and more. Out of idle politeness I commented on its good qualities. 'Glad you like it,' said Mr. Kyle, 'for it's all our own make.' Yes, he had made the boat single-handed, its oars and all its appurtenances. Here was Robinson Crusoe in person. I no longer regretted that my surroundings were not like England. Thankful that I had learnt to row in Wales, I offered to take an oar, and managed it to his satisfaction, but to the obvious terror of Mrs. Kyle, who feared the worst for her boy. Some distance up the creek we moored the boat so that I might be shown a pleasant walk among the woods. Here we came upon a splendid patch of wild raspberries, all ripe for eating, and the only check to our complete enjoyment was the constant cry to the boy not to eat too many.

A mill has always had a fascination for me since the days of my childhood when I loved to plunge my arms up to the elbows in the grain as it came rushing down the wooden shoot of the old Cornish mill. This Canadian mill was more modern in its methods, but doing just the same work. The miller's man seemed quite pleased to have an interested spectator, and showed me the flour in all its stages, and the precise purpose of each wheel. He allowed me to stencil names on the sacks, to fill a sack with flour, and to tie one up.

A day or two later Mr. Kyle brought in a mass of fish he had caught, chiefly perch and bass, and announcing that he was going into the yard to skin and clean them, asked me to come and help him. Mrs. Kyle was shocked at my being asked to do such a thing; but I was for trying everything I could, and readily joined him. It was nasty, dirty work, but I stuck to it. He then told me that I had made a great impression on the people round by merely enjoying myself, and that I had 'made a mash of the miller's man'. Mr. Kyle was a jolly companion, and as far as I was concerned he had only two drawbacks. One was that he measured the value of everything in dollars—the cost of a thing, that was always the main point, and sometimes I felt that if I heard the word dollar again I should scream. His other failing was to disparage everything English. No sooner did I speak of some building or process or improvement that I had seen lately in England than he would say, 'Oh, that's a back number; you should see what we have over here in Canada.' This annoyed me at first, and I argued the point, but his trick became so frequent that I either laughed or took no notice or heartily agreed with him. I discovered, to my amusement, that agreement with him annoyed him far more than contradiction. Once, when he had been particularly militant against England, I asked which of the poor old country's failings had driven him to Canada (where he had now been for twenty years). 'Rheumatism,' was his reply. 'But you have it very cold here in Canada, don't you?' said I. 'Cold, yes, but dry; not the damp cold I used to get at home. In England if you put clothes away dry they get wet, but in Canada if you put them away wet they get dry.' I felt sorry at the moment that I had made him recall his past illness, but that conversation explained a lot. I believe that at heart he was really homesick, and attacked everything English in order to hear me defend it. In a word, he was an exile, with the knowledge that a return would be a death sentence. In later years I have come to think that the world must be dotted over with poor fellows trying desperately to make out that the land of their adoption is superior to England.

One afternoon I felt bold enough to ask him if I might try my hand at fishing, when I saw him starting off for the creek with his tackle. Although I had watched it often enough I had never attempted it, supposing it far too sacred a business to be undertaken in a light spirit. I was at once supplied with the necessaries, and with beginner's luck I caught four good-

sized perch, while Mr. Kyle caught only one. I understood in
that blissful hour why it was that Dym and Arthur could spend
whole days at the job, dead to the world. With great pride I
carried them back to the hotel, cleaned them in the yard and
took them to the kitchen to be cooked for supper, when Mr.
Kyle duly advertised my success to the visitors. These consisted mostly of permanent boarders, interspersed with a few
'casuals'. On discovering quite a good piano in the dining-
room I suggested that we should have a dance one wet evening.
While they pushed aside the tables I struck up as lively a
measure as I knew, and soon they were all whirling round, and
to my amused astonishment I noted Mrs. Kyle having a turn
with the postman, who had been distracted from his round for
a minute or two!

Among the casual inhabitants one lunch-time was a stranger,
pointed out to me as 'Professor Cavanagh'. The idea of a
professor in such surroundings was odd in itself, and this one
had none of the hall-marks that one expects to see in a professor.

'What is he a professor *of*?' I asked Mrs. Kyle.

'Phrenology,' she whispered in a deferential tone. 'He
examines people's heads and reports on them for a dollar.'

When I laughed she added, 'Do be done; no one is coming
forward, and he wants a little encouragement.'

My dollars were getting dismally few, but I hadn't the heart
to refuse, and after lunch I asked to be 'done' and was solemnly
conducted to an empty room. He was young and cheery and
opened with a learned discourse on the relation of size of head
to brain power, with many an ancient saw and modern instance,
and sufficient statistics to convince the most sceptical. Among
these he had slightly emphasized the fact that 'a measurement
of less than nineteen inches indicates idiocy.' He then arranged
his instruments and proceeded to measure my head. 'Just eighteen and seven-eighths inches' he exclaimed in feigned distress.
I gave him the expected laugh, concluded that the whole affair
was to be an elaborate joke on such lines, and thought of
putting down in my accounts, 'To entertainment—1 dollar'.

But he assumed a more business-like air again after the laugh, and went on measuring this and that, and giving me quite sound advice without any compliments. I expect he had become pretty quick at deducing personal traits as he chatted with any one. He warned me against doing things in a hurry, such as jumping on moving cars and trying to do two things at once (thereby often giving myself more work). Hurry was my chief enemy, and I was specially to beware of spending money in a hurry, and of throwing good money after bad. If I could only have borne his good advice in mind it would have repaid me many times over the dollar I laid out for it.

My Londoner's love of shop-gazing led me inevitably to examine the few windows that Oakville displayed. One specially attracted me, for within I could see a cobbler in the act of making a pair of boots. After watching him in silence for some time I apologized for staring, and explained it as due to interest in his job. I had only to open my mouth to say anything in America to cause surprise and welcome at once. 'You come from England!' he exclaimed, 'Do you know Yorkshire?' I felt like saying with the indignant little French boy, when asked if he knew Paris, 'Si je connais Paris!' I soon persuaded him that I knew Yorkshire by talking familiarly of the main interests of York, Middlesbrough, Whitby, Saltburn, and lots of smaller places, including Danby Wiske (to his ecstasy). He had left his job to fetch out a Darlington and Stockton paper and a map of Yorkshire.

'Mrs. Nicolas, my wife here,' said he, calling her to come, 'is English too, only she won't admit it because she says the Cornish are not English.'

It was my turn for ecstasy. 'Cornish!' I cried, 'So am I. Where? What part? What was your name?'

When she said that she was a Curno of Lelant I could have fallen on her neck. Lelant! That most Cornish of Cornish villages, with its 'little grey church on a windy hill'. What with Yorkshire and Cornwall we had so much to say that they suggested my coming to tea with them on the following day. This seemed a good plan and I set off at four o'clock expecting a cup of tea and a long talk. The long talk was certainly provided, but instead of a 'cup of tea' there was a substantial meal laid in the tiny room at the back of the shop, and I saw why Mrs. Nicholas had required a day's interval for preparation. There was an uncut joint of cold beef with tomatoes, ripe raspberries and clotted cream, and the specially Cornish apple-cakes and saffron buns. Both she and her husband were bursting with hospitality and real affection. I promised to go to Lelant on my very first visit to Cornwall on my return, and I was entrusted with a pot of home-made jam to take to her mother. (I may add that all this I faithfully performed, and found old Mrs. Curno as warm-hearted as her daughter.)

Although I had turned my back on England for the time, I was glad enough of these happy links with it. The one thing entirely English that I would most willingly have forgone was the Canadian observance of Sunday. The church, of course, was a new nondescript building, to which I was led as a sheep to the slaughter by Mrs. Kyle, attired in her best bonnet and squeezed into gloves. Together we endured one of the dullest services of my wide experience in this line. When I remarked on it as we came out, and wondered why she didn't follow her husband's example and do a bit of meditating in the sun, she replied, 'I always go; it puts my conscience right and I feel that I have been blessed.' This sounded hopeful, and I reckoned that perhaps the afternoon would develop into some frivolity. But Mrs. Kyle preserved her pious demeanour, which generated a kind of truculence in her husband, and the afternoon yawned ahead. While she was reading a good book and forbidding her son to do whatever he was doing, Mr. Kyle approached me with an 'aside': 'What about a stroll down to the lake?' Off we went; he knew his Oakville; there was a hot sun and a stiffish breeze, the little port was alive with yachts, and all the abandoned portion of the village had come down to see what was going on. An expanse of blue water and a cloudless sky were all that nature had contributed to the scene, but Mr. Kyle exclaimed, 'Now this *is* a lake! Not like your little duckpond of a Windermere.' 'You are quite right,' I replied.

'I see no resemblance at all.' But just at that moment I saw right away on the horizon the foam of Niagara, being tossed up by the breeze, and called his attention to it with, *'There's* something to boast of, if you like!'

Presently we saw, in addition to the group of idlers admiring a huge catch of bass, a small company of earnest-looking people mustering at the water's edge. The word went round that they were Baptists about to hold a baptism. I had heard from a Baptist friend of mine that it was their custom to immerse the candidate entirely, and she had shown me the vast marble bath for the purpose in her chapel; but I had never really believed it. So now I watched eagerly to see what sort of compromise they made in actual practice. Two pastors and two candidates got into a rowing-boat and pushed off to a distance of about a hundred yards. They were all in mackintoshes, and sure enough the young people were ducked completely. Whatever of dignity might have conceivably been connected with this ritual under happier conditions was entirely absent in this case. To our disgust several of the local idlers had also got into boats and rowed out to jeer. We could only hope that the Baptists were too much absorbed in religious thoughts to be aware of what was going on around them.

The next day, in the evening, I had an attack of home-sickness, and while Mrs. Kyle was busy collecting her son and cajoling him to bed I looked round for some quiet corner to be by myself. The only available refuge, strangely, was the smoking-room. This was a gloomy den of a place, unpatronized by the men of the house, who smoked their vile pipes all over the hotel. Taking a book and the last letter I had received from Arthur I repaired to this little ark. The letter had been written in the Dolgelly Assize Court, where 'a case had been going on for hours that would have been knocked out in ten minutes up in London'. There were other things in the letter that made my home-sickness no better, so I thrust it back into its envelope and began to reckon how long it would be before I got back to Wales. Just then a man came in and sat down for a smoke. I was relieved to see that it was a cigarette—a rare thing in those surroundings. I was also relieved that he didn't start the usual immediate conversation, and relapsed into my dreams. After a while I was almost startled when the silence was broken by an Oxford voice:

'Excuse me, but is that an English stamp I glimpse on your letter?'

'Yes, it is,' said I, 'although it comes from Wales. Would you care to look at it more closely?' and I handed him the envelope.

'Thank you,' said he, 'that does me good, a real sight for sore eyes, for I'm suffering from a bout of home-sickness.'

When I confessed the same and how glad I was to smell a good cigarette and hear an English voice, we began to compare notes on this and that, and I was soon enjoying full compensation for Mr. Kyle's sneers at the old country. The stranger was a resident in Toronto, Mr. Arnold Haultain, private secretary to the well-known Goldwin-Smith (and later on his biographer). He said he was destined to be an exile for life, and an occasional visit to London was the utmost he could hope for. He envied me so much that I felt ashamed of making a grievance of my short absence. He was amused at my objection to Canada: its chief drawback, I maintained, was its likeness to England—you kept on expecting it to be English, and finding it only a caricature; whereas the States were original and full-blooded. He promised to send me some of his own literary work, articles on various subjects and poetry, and we agreed to meet in London on his next visit (which we did).

After we had exchanged cards he said, 'May I know what book you have on your lap? Or will it make me worse?'

'Worse, I fear; it's my pocket *Hamlet*. I take it everywhere with me as a kind of——'

'Prophylactic?'

At this we both laughed and launched forth into a discussion of our common literary tastes. It grew dark, and he rose to go; pausing at the door, he turned round and said with a courtly bow, 'For this relief, much thanks'.

§ 2

The time was come for me to rejoin my travelling companion at Toronto, and Mr. Kyle escorted me over the lake in order to show me 'the finest town in the world'. I fell in with all his opinions, freely admitting that the main street was far larger and grander than Regent Street. In spite of his absurd adulation I found it a beautiful town. We took a five-cent belt-line trip right round it, if the word 'round' is correct, for all arrangement in America seems to be square. The special charm to me was the openness of the private gardens. No fences or hedges or walls anywhere. 'Don't small boys pick the flowers?' I asked, and Mr. Kyle explained that no one stole the flowers or trampled the grass plots because every citizen acted as a policeman. I thought how much pleasure our suburban gardens might give to town dwellers if we did away with our excluding barriers, not to mention the ugly iron railings round the London squares.

We had a bit of business to do in the town. Mr. Kyle had insisted that I must go back to England first class, and indeed I was only too willing to be persuaded; so we changed my second cabin ticket for a saloon on the *New York*. After this effort we had lunch in a style quite new to me; we sat on high stools at a long counter and had a great variety of funny dishes to choose from. Dutiful visits to Dr. Ross's Normal School and the University, and a row on the lake brought the day to an end with meeting my friend at the Queen's Hotel, and a farewell to Mr. Kyle.

Our plan was to go to Quebec, and next morning early we took ship in the *Spartan*, quite appropriately named as it turned out. My imagination had been running riot over the 'Thousand Isles'. One of my childish dreams of delight had been to live on a little Island, with neighbours all around on similar islands, to step into my boat to pay a call or do shopping or just potter about. I understood that the part of the river we were to pass through was dotted with such ideal residences, and that we should see the people pottering about in their boats. To my bitter disappointment it was a day of drenching rain. Not a lift all day. The saloon was not pleasant, so we sat on deck huddled up in rugs and mackintoshes. The ship's dinner was too spartan to arouse appetite. However, there was still the shooting of the Lachine Rapids to come, and that was better even than the islands. 'The rapids are near and the day-light's past'—the words were running in my head when the news went round that the evening was too dark for shooting the rapids! It was the first day that this had happened for the whole season. We were all bundled out at a railway station, but as there was no train, nor hope of one, we were all bundled in again, to be taken to Montreal by the canal. This meant a far longer time, and the *Spartan* had no meal provided for the now hungry passengers. This was the last straw in a day of disappointments. But, as it happened, it proved to be one of the merriest of my experiences. A 'free supper' was proclaimed, and every morsel of food on board was brought forth, and served round in the saloon with the impartial justice of a survival from shipwreck. Our appetites were no longer nice, every one was good-tempered, and even the stewards laughed at our gratitude for a bun or a potato that we should have despised earlier in the day. I remember the excellence of an orange that fell to my share.

Since everything was out of order, there was great con-fusion on the wharf when we arrived at Montreal, and for some time the gangway couldn't be got across. We drove to the Quebec-going wharf only to find that our boat had already started. So we took the C.P.R. night train, curled up in a day car, and fell fast asleep. How queer it was to see Quebec written up on a board, as if it were no more than some suburban station. We took a *calèche* to the Florence Hotel, and spent the day prowling about the strange ups and downs of the old town. The breakneck steps and the curious old shops, where one had to ask for things in French—this was the real Canada that I had wanted to see. Fortunately I was able to go exactly where I liked, for my friend had lost one of her many trunks in the con-fusions of the previous day and was absorbed in inquiries for it.

The following morning at breakfast, while we were discussing which of the many historical places we should go to
see on the one day at our disposal, two Yankees at an adjoining
table overheard our remarks, came up to us and said that they
too were on a short visit, didn't know where to go, and would
we join them if they hired a carriage and told the man to drive
us round to some interesting spots? My friend was obviously
suspicious of the arrangement and put up a strong case that she
really ought to be making further endeavours to find her missing trunk. 'Oh, bother your trunk,' said I, 'come along and
forget it.' I hustled her off to get ready while the carriage was
being ordered. 'I think we are very unwise,' said she, 'to accept
a favour from these vulgar men.' 'They aren't vulgar,' said I,
'they are just real Yankees come here for a holiday like us.
They are obviously well off, and we shall afford them entertainment merely by being so different from themselves; I expect
that's why they asked us.'

Certainly I got immense amusement from watching them on
our drive. It was my first close-up acquaintance with the real
article of which I had heard and read so much. Their tone of
voice was the richest twang I had come across; they had goatee
beards, diamond breast-pins, and rings, and addressed one
another as Doctor and Colonel. They smoked strong cigars
the whole time and, of course, spat freely. As I looked at them
I didn't believe it—it was all too much like the comic papers.
I chatted away to them, in order to make up for my friend's
rather reserved manner; but there was no need, for I think they
were amply amused and pleased with her, no doubt thinking
that they had encountered a genuine specimen of the real stand-
offish English lady.

The morning excursion was to the Montmorency Falls, where
the 'doctor' and I ventured to the foot, down steep, slippery
wooden steps that had lately given way, and were rather crazy.
It was a cloudy morning with some rain, but the good lunch to
which we were entertained and a sunny afternoon put us in
capital spirits as we drove to the Plains of Abraham. Here we
saw one of the most moving monuments in the world, the

column with 'Wolfe' inscribed on one side, and 'Montcalm' on the other. It meant a lot to us, but the Yankees 'didn't just remember what battle that was'. Still more interesting to me was to see the cove where Wolfe climbed up so stealthily, but it meant nothing at all to the Yankees. They may not have known much history, but they certainly knew how to be hospitable to strangers, and we parted from them with warm thanks.

We hated having to leave Quebec, but we were due to take ship that evening for Montreal. The St. Lawrence was looking superb in the summer evening light, as we sat on deck admiring the broad expanse of calm water and the wooded banks. A special dinner at the captain's table was followed by a tour of the vessel, including the engine-room, conducted by the captain himself. Then one of the passengers showed me a copy of *Puck*, explaining the jokes I didn't understand and also those I did. I thought it a good name for a comic paper, but didn't think that its contents lived up to it. I went to my bunk reluctantly, sorry to waste any part of the journey along the St. Lawrence in sleep, and was up early to greet Montreal.

Sunday morning was an appropriate time to arrive in the 'city of churches' and we sampled several of them, including Notre Dame, the Jesuits' church, the Wesleyan church, and the English cathedral, staying for a part of the service in each. In the cathedral they sang my favourite *Te Deum*, which had the extra charm of the familiar amid strange surroundings. After this the sermon in the Wesleyan place was a painful drop, and we didn't stay to hear it through.

In the afternoon we were able to understand the beautiful meaning of the word 'Montreal', for we went for a drive up the Royal Mount, and through the Catholic and Protestant cemeteries. It dawned on me then why there were so many churches in the city—doubtless owing to the rivalry between the many sects, even more numerous than at home. But up on the Mount we were above them all, and could *see* the whole city as I have never seen one before or since. It was a gentle hazy mass of red houses, interspersed with trees and the slender church spires. Beyond was the St. Lawrence. Odd bits of geography lessons, so dull at school, came to my mind. I had learnt that the St. Lawrence carries more water to the sea than any other river, and so might be called the greatest in the world, and I looked on its calm expanse with awe. And what a lovely setting the city had! Beyond the great river with its wooded islands was a richly cultivated plain and in the distance were blue and grey hills. The river was spanned by an unbelievably long bridge (our driver said it was 'going on for two miles'). Altogether it was a scene to remember for a lifetime. I wished I had taken my sketch-book with me, but had to be content with a rough impression of the city that I managed to get from the window of our St. Lawrence Hall Hotel.

We had only one more day, and I was determined to shoot the Lachine Rapids. I could never go home and say I had missed them in a paltry canal. With difficulty I persuaded my friend to go with me by a Grand Trunk train and return on the steamer. I hoped it would take her mind off the trunk anxiety, which neither the voyage on the St. Lawrence nor the cathedral service nor the view from the Royal Mount had been able to allay. 'After all,' said I, 'it's only one small trunk that you have lost. Why not enjoy a little life while the poor thing is trying to reach you?'

I wouldn't have missed that shooting of the rapids for anything. It's true that I had always pictured the 'shooting' in a canoe, with a Red Indian captain, but the steamer was quite exciting enough. It plunged along light-heartedly over appalling places, and several times I was certain that it simply *must* strike the rock at which it was aiming directly—but no, it glanced off miraculously just at the fateful moment. It may have been inconvenient for navigation that the river took it into its head to narrow in this part, but it provided no end of fun. We now had a closer view of the great tubular bridge, as we slid peacefully under it after the hazards of the rapids. Although it had been built so strong in order to resist the flow of water and the pressure of ice at one season of the year, it looked to me as if it might come down any minute. Indeed, the rapids seemed safer.

'We haven't done our duty in the educational line here,' I
said, as we were spending the afternoon in a final stroll round
the town. 'Let's ask this clergyman to show us something of
the kind.' He was only too pleased, and took us over M'Gill
College. It was not term time, but we saw some fine apparatus
for scientific experiments in the technological school, and we
were supplied with information and papers about the University. As though in reward for our dutiful afternoon we found
on return to the hotel that the lost trunk had arrived. At once
its owner was all smiles and apologies for the ill-temper she
had shown during the period when the little trunk had been
off by itself. But, funnily enough, her rejoicing enraged me
more than her previous gloom, for it was out of all proportion
to the event. I had had enough of her and her trunk. Breaking
to her that my passage home had been altered, I told her that
I should not travel with her that night, but go by a different
route on the following morning. I went to see her off by the
C.P.R. and I suppose my cheerfulness broke through, for she
said, 'I believe you are glad that I'm leaving you.' Knowing
that truth is the greatest deceiver I replied gaily, 'Yes, indeed
I am.' She was a good bit older than I, and consequently was
full of compunction at leaving me alone on the continent.
'Alone on the continent!' The idea went to my head like wine.
I was free. I laughed on my way back to the hotel at the absurdity of having all America to play about in. For a first venture
from England this seemed good.

V

Boston, Mass.

WHILE parting so gaily from my fellow traveller I was hugging to myself a plan. I would spend a few days of those left, before my boat was due to sail, in a visit to Boston.

My 'knowledge' of Canada had received continual rebuffs, but then it was a huge tract of country, whereas Boston was only one town, and I really did know a good deal about it. It was more familiar to English ears than New York itself. Called after the little seaport of Boston, Lincs., it had far out-shone its godfather, and many a letter intended for England had gone over to Boston, Mass. The point that tickled me most was that Boston was 'not in America'. The ultra-exclusive inhabitants were neither English nor American, but just Bostonians—*sui generis*.. I was eager to hear the special kind of accent they had developed. It was also a pleasure to know that the town could not be laid out in the chess-board style of Chicago. The streets were so narrow and in-and-out that a man had been known to catch his own coat-tails in hurrying round a corner. And yet the town must be modern and busy, for the legend ran that they killed a man a day in the traffic. Altogether a most alluring spot. If a bit medieval here and there, that was appropriate, because this Botolph's town had been named after a kindly East Anglian saint who protected travellers. Indeed, in old days a prayer and small donation to St. Botolph were an insurance for your journey. I didn't appeal to him but to the next best thing to a saint, a kindly fellow guest at the hotel in Montreal. He recommended the route through the White Mountain district, and perhaps he was inspired by St. Botolph, for it was a heavenly journey from first to last.

Neither knowing nor caring how long the journey would be, I put into my hold-all a few things that experience had taught

me might be handy as I went along, and checked my trunk to
Boston. I wondered how my friend could ever have lost a
package of any kind, since this system of checking was simplicity itself—you cared not how your luggage got on, nor what
route it took—it was bound to find its fellow check in due
course, and you had that in your pocket.

After an early start from Montreal there was a midday
change at a place called Johnsburg (as well as I remember).
Here was a chance for a refreshing wash, a sandwich, and a
glass of milk. Apparently it was a border station, and when
we started in the train that came up we were in the States. It is
difficult to say why I was so pleased to be under the stars and
stripes again; it seemed as vaguely attractive as being entirely
by myself, I had to be neither submissive nor loyal. I now
settled down for a good long run to Boston, put on slippers
and travelling cap, and placed a book handy for reading, but
found the scenery getting ever more interesting as the train
wound among the hills. I was feeling at the acme of comfort,
when by came the conductor to examine tickets. There were
few passengers in the car, so he was in no hurry and seemed
inclined for a chat.

'What time this evening do we reach Boston?' I asked.

'This evening! We shan't get there this evening at all.'

'A night in the train?' said I in dismay. 'Why, that will
mean missing all this beautiful scenery.'

'Well, if that's what you want, why not spend the night
somewhere on the way, and go on to-morrow by daylight?'
Then pulling out his list of stations he added, 'Look here,
Fabyans is a·fine spot, and a good hotel there and all. I could
put you ashore there.'

'Good hotel! But my trunk is checked on to Boston, and
I've only this little hold-all. I can't possibly put up like this at
a decent hotel.'

'Oh, don't you mind about clothes. They're all just holiday
people there. You settle down again comfortably; I'll tell
you when to get ready to jump out—about four o'clock.'

For the next two hours we ran through distractingly lovely

country, all too fast, now through woods, now across wild moorland, now pushing a way through hedges so close that they brushed the windows; indeed at one time I thought we should be caught in the branches. And all around were hills. The sun was shining and fleecy clouds were throwing shadows in a way that reminded me of Wales.

Was there an hotel at Fabyans! There was nothing else. The railway station was its front door. I was the only passenger to get out. The train was off at once, and I had no choice but to go in. The word 'holiday-makers' had suggested a little wayside shanty, with the minimum of amenities, and people in camping outfit—and a couple of dollars the amount of the bill. To my surprise and distress I walked into a magnificent lounge, decorated expensively with ferns, flowers, flags, and festoons, as though for some gala occasion. A huge log fire was crackling in the grate, and rest-inviting chairs were scattered about. The many people talking and laughing about the place were of a type I had not seen before in America, obviously both wealthy and cultivated, all well dressed, but quite simply, and every one seemed care-free and jolly. How awkward I felt, standing in the entrance watching them—me with my ridiculous hold-all and travel-stained clothes. Seeing a little office at one side I went up to the reception clerk, told him plainly my predicament, and holding out a gold piece said that I expected he would like to be paid in advance as I had no luggage. He was shocked at such an idea, and had me conducted at once to a dainty little room with a fine view of the hills. The chambermaid informed me that hot baths were always to be had, and meals were served continually in the dining-room, to suit the various holiday outings of the guests, and then she asked whether I wanted anything else.

I didn't tell her so, but my wants were many. I turned out my hold-all to see what could be done. In addition to the slippers and cap and small toilet necessities, there was little beyond the inevitable *Hamlet*, my sketching-book and paint-box, and the book I had bought to read in the train and neglected (*A Window in Thrums*). But fortunately I found in one of the pockets a needle-case, and was glad enough of it, for I had torn my sleeve in one of my excited movements across the railway car to see a view. After mending this I made a sketch of the hills to be seen from the window, and then was driven by hunger to overcome my shyness and look for a meal in the dining-room. A very friendly waitress served me immediately with a supper I shall never forget: salmon, chicken (with all sorts of small attendant dishes), griddle-cakes with clover honey, and real tea, such as I hadn't enjoyed since leaving home.

The beautiful evening tempted me out for a stroll along the hill-paths and through the pine-wood behind the hotel. Then I sat on the grass and tried to impress the scene on my memory —and succeeded. Everything combined to make it memorable, although each item by itself was familiar—mountains all round and a white mist in the valley, the dark pines, the rising moon, and one brilliant star—such things any one may see. But other items in the scene, equally familiar, gave a unique touch to it. The lovely green and red signal lights I had often admired outside King's Cross station; but here they twinkled like fire-flies. Little mountain trains I had known in Wales, but here great thundering expresses were hurtling through, with enormous funnels, horn-blowing and bell-ringing in the misty valley. One engine-driver's face looked weird in the glow of his fire, and reminded me of the steersman in the most haunting line of the *Ancient Mariner*. It grew dark and I reluctantly went indoors—to find another surprise. Half the floor of the big hall had been cleared for dancing and a string band was playing, interspersed with singing in which the dancers joined. Acutely conscious of my everyday dress, rendered worse by my poor mend of the sleeve and my walk in the wood, I found a secluded chair and hoped to escape notice. I would have gone up to my room had I not found the scene too amusing and the music too intoxicating. Very soon some one came up to me and begged for a dance. I couldn't resist and quickly forgot my dress in that merry and friendly crowd.

The next morning, as I was waiting in the lounge for my

train to come up, I noticed parties of young men and girls standing about in groups, all of them equipped for going up the mountains. 'You're not *going*!' they exclaimed. 'You mustn't miss the chance of such a perfect day as this for the mountains.' When I pleaded the shortness of my time before sailing for England, they said, 'But this is the Switzerland of America. Risk missing your boat. Cut Boston short. Come right along with us now.' If ever my mouth watered it did then, but my slender purse had already endured big inroads. . . . The many follies I've committed in life don't cause me half as much regret as the follies I never tasted.

My new train had an observation car at the rear, where the passengers were crowded; but they were most courteous in making room for the new-comer, and in pointing out and naming the places of interest. The views of the White Mountains, and especially of Crawford Notch, made me regret still more my not having made the ascent; but I was grateful enough to that conductor who had saved me from passing such delights in the night-train.

A fifteen minutes' stop at a wayside halt doesn't sound pleasant. There was no town near, nor anything. But I have never come across such a dream of a refreshment-room. The bar was loaded with freshly cut sandwiches (not deadly similar within), new buns, an enticing variety of cakes, huge pears, oranges, and jugs of creamy milk. I compared it with our English refreshment-rooms, usually so stale, dirty, and graceless. I understood Dickens's description of the American at Mugby Junction: 'I la'af. I dew. I la'af at yewer fixins, solid and liquid.' More than forty years have passed since I had that wayside meal, and yet an American would still laugh at our rock cakes and coffee essence and other miseries. Dickens's satire had no success in this direction.

I don't think there was any scheduled time for this pleasant stop, but when the conductor thought we had had enough to eat and finished our rambling round the engine and chat with the driver, he said, without raising his voice, 'All aboard,' and we all climbed in.

Glancing at the heading of a fellow passenger's book, I saw 'Sensation in General', guessed it was psychology, and expressed sympathy with her; we then exchanged ideas on teaching, and she told me of a plan being tried in her school for getting children to write quickly; they would copy some simple letter, say *o*, to the tune of 'Bonny Dundee' played on the piano, over and over again without lifting their pens from the page. I still think this a more useful exercise than the awkward script writing, which is often illegible and never rapid.

It was with real excitement that I jumped out at Boston, found my trunk, and took a hurdy to one of the hotels on Cook's list. A plan of the town was lent me, and I ventured on a short stroll in the hour before dinner. Now the unexpected thing about Boston was that (unlike Canada) it was just what I expected. Indeed, in that first stroll I nearly contributed my bit to the casualty statistics, for I was crossing a seemly looking road, quite naturally endowed with rails, when I was aware of a huge truck towering over me and backing on to me. I skipped off just in time, but returned to the hotel a bit shaken. It was hardly reassuring to read on the notice-board in the entrance-hall that 1,600 cars passed the doors daily—intended as a recommendation. Boston was obviously a busy town. Labour-saving too. The number of bedrooms was enormous, and the service was managed by a curious scheme to avoid double journeys. I found hung up in my room a list of all that man could reasonably want, and opposite each, the number of pings on the bell that would bring it: 1 ping, the boot-boy; 2 pings, iced water; 3 pings, hot water; and so on up to 15 pings. What the 15 would bring I can't remember—that it was the fire-brigade was a later suggestion of Arthur's. Anyhow I was so alarmed lest I should ping too many or too few that I satisfied all my wants quite quietly by hunting about the hotel. The negro waiters and my fellow guests were very helpful when I needed assistance, especially in finding my way to the various places of interest in the neighbourhood.

My first objective was Boxford, a little village near Salem,

to see Professor Palmer, of Harvard, to whom I had an introduction. I had written to say I was coming, and set out early
on my first morning by train for Boxford. The station-master
greeted me and explained that Mr. Palmer was at work all the
morning and couldn't come himself, but had given orders that
I was to be driven to his house. Then helping me to a seat in
a gig he jumped up and took the reins himself. 'But surely,'
said I, 'you are not going to leave your station to look after
itself?' 'Oh, yes, there won't be another train for a couple of
hours.' Our way was along a deeply wooded lane that might
have been dropped straight out of Devon, but the pine forest
that came next was too dark and sinister-looking for anything
I had seen at home. I almost expected to hear the howl of a
wolf. It was 'New England' but seemed to me more like what
one might imagine the 'Old England' of a thousand years ago.

The house was a dream of a place, an old cottage of historical interest (I forget exactly what, for every place around
Boston had some bit of history connected with it). Mrs.
Palmer was at the open door with arms extended to welcome
me. In spite of August weather she had a wood fire 'just to
add warmth to my greeting', she explained. On the fire was
a kettle, and tea was at once made for me, 'for I know how
English people love tea at any hour.' 'Well, this is my first
Boston Tea Party,' said I, 'and I little thought when I learnt
about it at school in what lovely surroundings I should drink
tea in Boston.' At the midday dinner that soon followed
Professor Palmer joined us and between the two of them I
learnt a great deal more about education in America than I
had gleaned from the Conference. They were not striving to
impress me or be uplifting, but were refreshingly critical.
Mr. Palmer was a friend of William James, the only human
writer on psychology that I had come across. While we were
chatting I suddenly remembered the boast of the Bostonians
that they were not American. So perfectly English was their
accent that I didn't notice it! Perhaps it would have escaped
me altogether if I hadn't been brought sharp up against one
slip on the part of Mrs. Palmer. Mr. Palmer was perfect, but I

found the Achilles heel in his wife. She said how vurry pleased she was about something. It gave me quite a little shock of pleasure to hear it. I felt like saying, 'Et tu, Brute?'

Cambridge and Harvard College were naturally the next places for me to visit, and I started off by tram very early in order to see as much as possible before the midday heat. The conductor of the tram was angry with me for jumping off before it stopped, and still more angry when I laughed. A little boy immediately stepped up to me and offered to tell me which building was which. He looked to me as if he had only recently been put into breeches, but he seemed to know his way around. A kindly little fellow, I thought, probably filling in a dull holiday-time. He didn't appear to belong to the well-to-do class (although one could never be sure), and I wondered whether he would be offended by a tip. So after a quarter of an hour's amble round I compromised by thanking him and giving him a quarter to 'buy sweets'. Offended he certainly was. Rejecting my coin with scorn he demanded two dollars as his proper fee! Walking away I left him to pick up his tip or leave it, as the fancy struck him.

I said that Boston fulfilled my expectations in every particular, but Cambridge and Harvard outran them. With visions of Chicago University in my mind I was afraid of imagining anything too glowing, and was therefore delightfully disappointed. Creeper-clad Old Massachusetts Hall took my fancy immensely, reminding me of many a college building in our own Cambridge; and the funny name fascinated me too. So I sat on the grass and tried to get an impression of it in my sketch-book, grumbling at my lack of colours for the brilliant green of the creeper, and still more at my lack of skill to do the trees. Absorbed in my job, I was shocked to hear an 'English' lady's voice behind me, 'Allow me to remove this bug from your neck.' It was only a harmless little fly, and we both laughed at my acquiring a new American usage.

Longfellow as a poet I had long outgrown, but always had happy associations with verses learnt in childhood, and felt it an act of piety to visit his house. They had made a museum of his study, crowding it with such absurd mementoes as a chair 'made from the wood of the spreading chestnut-tree'. A far more appropriate relic of the poet was a portrait of Keats, the well-known one by Severn. I asked the attendant whether it had been hung there by Longfellow himself, and she supposed it had, for it had been in the same place as long as she could remember. This specially interested me, since Arthur possessed a similar copy of the portrait, given to him by Walter Severn, the son of the artist.

It was not Lowell's poetry but his *Biglow Papers* that led me to pay respects to his grave—a very simple one. The *Biglow Papers* were in verse, of course, but it was their humour that mother and I had enjoyed so much. How she used to roll over her tongue,

> *But John P.*
> *Robinson he*
> *Said they didn't know everything down in Judee.*

A visit to Bunker's Hill and mounting to the top of the monument, and efforts to remember details of the war with America (treated vaguely in school days), consumed the afternoon, and I returned hot and thirsty to the hotel, alarming the negro waiter by the amount of tea I drank. The heat was so great that one could neither sit nor lie nor stand, like the prisoners in the Bastille.

Next morning I was up early again and took a seven-something train to Wellesley, walked up to the College through a beautiful lane and park, to be greeted and shown over the buildings by Mrs. Case. On my return I felt that I had heard enough about education for a long time, and might indulge in my own fancies for the rest of my stay in America. At one period I had idolized Emerson, and in spite of the gruelling heat I went off in the afternoon by railway to Concord. I walked to Sleepy Hollow (what a marvellous name to imagine) and there came across Rip himself. Glad of any excuse to speak to the aged fellow, I asked him to show me which was Emerson's grave. This was certainly a pleasing contrast to Longfellow's study, for the only memorial was a huge boulder. For that little pilgrimage I hadn't peas in my shoes, but suffered nobly enough. Scarcely able to drag myself along the dusty road to the depot, yet hurrying in the hope of just catching a train, I found myself with nearly an hour to wait. The only bright spot in the desolate little booking-office was the notice: 'No smoking. Especially pipes.' I saw plenty of Massachusetts on the return journey, for it was the slowest train that I have ever experienced. When I sank into bed that night I determined to *do* no more sights, but to see Boston as any town ought to be seen, by walking about aimlessly, and let Boston make its own impression.

Accordingly next morning I ventured out without my map, feeling sure that I knew Boston now, and having the Londoner's dislike of being seen consulting a map in the street and being thought a tourist. Delighting in my freedom from both education and interesting sights, I pranced down street after street, muttering to myself a line from what I always considered the perfect holiday poem, especially for a teacher who endured 'supervision duty':

Dorm on the herb, with none to supervise.

What was my astonishment when my eyes fell on the house of their author. Thrice blessed are the 'sights' that we run against accidentally. I stared; it was true; on a little creeper-covered house of no apparent importance was a small brass plate with the magic name O. W. Holmes. No doubt the actual autocrat was inside, possibly sounding somebody's chest or making up a prescription. I went to and fro, and then close up to the bell, and had the greatest difficulty in resisting the impulse to ring and ask to see the doctor about some imaginary complaint. I had no possible symptom of anything, and dragged myself away. How often I have since wished that I had rung that bell, asked to see him, and simply told him of the pleasure his books had given me.

I did the next best thing, looked about for a bookshop, asked to see his works, and bought a copy of the one which a false friend had borrowed and not returned. The man in

the shop was the only unpleasant American I struck. Perhaps
it was the heat, for he was obviously in a bad temper. As
he wrapped up the book he remarked surlily, 'You English
people! You all go down on your knees to a lord.' 'Do we?'
said I as though seeking information, 'I never noticed that.'
'Oh yes,' he went on, 'you grovel to them.' I said I had missed
the grovelling act, but he was so cross and earnest that I
thought it better not to laugh or contradict, so bowing my
head at last in solemn acquiescence I went off. After a leisurely
lunch in a cool-looking café, I thought I would make my way
gradually back to the hotel by a new route. It was certainly
a new route and certainly gradual. I had wandered and turned
about so much during the morning that I had lost all sense of
direction, and had no idea where my hotel was. I found that
its name, 'The United States Hotel', made no impression on
the people I asked. They couldn't rightly just say where it was.
Even when I mentioned to one man that 1,600 cars passed its
doors daily he only smiled. I began to see that the chess-board
arrangement of Chicago had some advantages, and even the
dreadful numbering of the streets. I could see no post-office.
I was too good a Londoner to speak to a policeman on traffic
duty, but at last I spied one who was seemingly at leisure for
the moment—a fine, tall fellow, in the cool garments and light
helmet that our bobbies would envy. I approached him with,
'Can you tell me where the United States Hotel is, officer?'
'It's where it was yesterday!' he snapped, not to be trifled with.
But when I looked bewildered he melted, and pointing with
a smile across the road said, 'Over there.' Boston, thought I,
is Looking-glass Land to the life—you can't reach a place, but
walk away from it and you bump into it.

The next day was my last and a Sunday, and I meant to
keep cool and not go far afield, to put pride in my pocket and
take a map. I made for a church 'noted for its fine services',
but found that they were taking far too long to ask the Lord to
have mercy on them, considering the state of the weather.
Then I tried another 'noted for architecture' and went in only
to find the same petitions going on, but at a later stage. I had

given up the idea of attending any service at all when I noticed a building whose excessive architecture proclaimed it to be something non-conforming. 'Anything for a change,' thought I, and walked in to find a sermon impending. I should have hurriedly withdrawn, but a kindly man ushered me to a seat and I found myself in the midst of a large and hearty congregation. A big fellow in a black gown was on a kind of platform, and in front of him an open Bible cushioned on a desk. After a significant pause he began to prance to and fro, and announced from various positions on the platform: 'One thing thou lackest' (which I took to be his text). 'Here,' said he, 'we have a fine building, one of the very finest in our country' (elaboration of its merits followed). 'We have all the best appointments—comfortable pews, good ventilation, stained-glass windows' (more elaborations of each). 'Our splendid and costly organ, raised by our own efforts, is now free of debt' (this surprised me). 'I may say without boasting that our choir can beat any in Boston' (recent successes in competitions enumerated). 'We have an overflowing congregation. Owing to your generosity we have had the means to do all this.' Here followed another long pause, and I made sure that all this was to lead up to an appeal for dollars for a new vestry-room or some such excrescence. 'One thing thou lackest,' he said in a low, quiet tone, as he seemed to eye each one of us. Then suddenly, with a business-like jerk of the head, he finished with, 'All we want now is the Holy Ghost to run the show.'

At my last meal before leaving that evening a woman at my table ate as much like a pig as any one can. I counted ten little dishes arranged around her, and even so her vegetable was on the cloth. What a town of extremes, and I felt that in my short stay I had been lucky enough to see a good many of them.

> *Here's to, the city of Boston,*
> *The home of the bean and the cod,*
> *Where the Lowells speak only to Cabots,*
> *And the Cabots speak only to God.*

VI

Meeting the Sun

JUST before leaving Boston I had a letter from my late travelling companion warning me of all the dangers of New York. 'On no account take a cab. I had to pay six dollars for mine.' I pictured the scene with some amusement—the cabby's revenge for the many trunks and a haughty manner. I forget the other pitfalls of the city, but thought it would be wise to check my one trunk straight through to the hotel, and so be independent of cabs. My route lay by train to Fall River and thence by boat to New York. It was dark when I went aboard; I was dirty and tired with the train journey, and had to wait ages in a queue to see the purser, to get a state-room. When at last my turn came the only thing left was to share a cabin with five others. One sight of these quarters was enough to keep me from bed as long as possible, and I amused myself by prolonging my dinner and watching my fellow passengers. The S.S. *Plymouth* was said to be the finest of its kind afloat, and it seemed to be used for pleasure trips, for although it looked already full enough, lots more people came aboard at a port where we called; and there followed the gayest scenes of music and dancing in the saloon. Driven by fatigue to my berth I had a miserable night, and when we docked in the morning I felt too weak and faint to get about. Turning resolutely from the inviting cabs, I induced a car to stop for me, and reached the haven of the Broadway Central Hotel. After a bath and breakfast and a couple of hours' sleep I felt equal to anything.

There was no time to waste, for in two days my boat sailed. A little business had to be done first, including a visit to the post-office for letters, and another to Cook's to get my money changed. How pleasing were the English sovereigns and pennies. I kept only enough American money for immediate needs, except one gold piece which I put away carefully (and still possess) as a memento of so jolly a visit. Even these short walks exhausted me, for New York exhibited a kind of heat completely new to me. Boston had been hot, but here there was a dry, choking heat, as though one were being smothered in blankets. I even longed for the Atlantic, and I can't put it more strongly than that. I discarded as many clothes as I could, and understood Sidney Smith's desire to take off his skin and sit in his bones. In addition to the heat the noise of the street was terrific, although the traffic in Broadway was anything but enormous as compared with Oxford Street or Holborn. The paving consisted of those big stones (about the size of an ordinary brick) that used to make travel in the buses of old days so sickening, and that have now been discarded in London. Some one in the hotel explained to me that the extremes of heat and frost in New York defied any attempt at better paving. But I expect that by now something has been done to counteract the noise.

No more walking that day for me, and I spent the afternoon in a twenty-five cent drive round Central Park, feeling sorry for the Americans that they had not such grand old trees as we have in Kensington Gardens. One road I was particularly anxious to see—Fifth Avenue. This I had always understood to be the home of millionaires and the intellectual and social *élite* of New York. I expected a super-magnificent Park Lane. I went along it, and said to myself, is this really it? No doubt there is more than meets the eye.

And now only one more day in America, and all New York to choose from. I was quite certain what my choice would be. I meant to go to see the Stock Exchange, weather or no. My father had told me little bits about the London Stock Exchange, and I knew that no outsider could enter its holy precincts. To this day I am fond of going down Throgmorton regions and watching all the busy to-ing and fro-ing in the street, picturing my father among them. Well, I understood that the New York exchange was not so exclusive, and that any one might go up into the gallery at Wall Street and look down on the brokers broking. I had heard that they did a good deal of

shouting, but the scene exceeded my wildest fancies. The
yelling and the gestures were a blend of the lion-house, the
monkey-house, and the parrot-house in the Zoo. There was
only one other spectator in the gallery, and presently I remarked
to him that the citizens of New York were missing a splendid
entertainment. He looked at me in a puzzled way, and then
said, 'It's new to you. You are a stranger, you're English,
aren't you?' I admitted it, and he added, 'Well, we don't think
anything of this; they're just doing ordinary business; it's a
dull day—a darned slack day. You must come again when
there's something really going on.' 'Unfortunately I'm sailing
to-night,' I replied, 'so there will be no other chance.' 'Then
I hope you have had a good time and seen plenty.' I laughed
as I told him that I had only two days for New York, and so
far had seen only Central Park, Fifth Avenue, and the Stock
Exchange. 'Come with me now,' said he, 'and I will show you
as much as possible in ten minutes.' He then took me to the
top of the Equitable building, whence there was a view of the
whole city. 'You can tell them way back,' said he, 'that you saw
all of New York.' Unfortunately all I can remember now is the
statue of Liberty, which I had already seen sufficiently, but my
friend gave me statistics of the number of people who could
dine in her head, or something equally absurd. It made my
arm ache to look at that statue, and I realized why a piece of
sculpture should never give one a restless sensation.

For my last afternoon I went for a stroll, but was careful
not to stray too far from my base, lest I should get lost again.
Even so, I soon became exhausted with the heat, and thought
I would go back on the elevated railroad. Spying a little book-
ing-office I asked for a ticket to the nearest station to my hotel.
'Five cents,' said the clerk, as he slapped down the ticket.
Searching my purse I found that I had come out without any
small change.

'Sorry,' said I, handing back the ticket, 'I'm afraid I
must walk back. I've no money on me except an English
sovereign.'

'Oh, do let me look at it!' cried the clerk, and when I handed it to him he gazed on it as in a trance, and then said, 'I'm English, too.'

'What part of England do you come from?' I asked.

'A place called Manchester,' said he. 'Do you know it?'

'Do I know it!' I laughed. 'Why, every one knows Manchester. I'm only a Londoner, and the saying is that what Manchester thinks to-day London thinks to-morrow.'

He thereupon thrust my sovereign and the ticket back to me, and said it didn't matter about the five cents. We managed to shake hands through the little booking-hole.

I was quite glad to get back into the shelter of the hotel, for the weather had developed a terrifically high wind, a sort of sirocco. I amused myself by making a pen-and-ink drawing of Broadway from the veranda, then packed my hold-all and watched the scenes in the street until dusk, when it was time to start for the boat. My trunk had been sent on, so that I had nothing to do but make my way to the docks by car. Again I had that queer feeling of the unreality of the whole thing—stepping out of an hotel and boarding an Atlantic liner so casually.

The S.S. *New York* was a palatial affair compared to the *Adriatic*. I had a roomy cabin all to myself (an advantage impossible to overrate), and as soon as I had disposed of my things I wandered about to explore the vessel. Presently it occurred to me that it was rather cold-blooded to leave a country where I had been treated so hospitably without saying good-bye to some one. Seeing a young officer, I said, 'Which way is it to the sea, please?' When he laughed I explained that it was not exactly the sea that I wanted, but to find the place where I could get ashore. Then I ran across the gangway on to America again. It was now quite dark, but not far away I saw the glare of some stalls. I bought two large pears, and astonished the man by telling him that I was all alone, was just off to England, and wanted to say good-bye to him. When I added that I felt hungry but couldn't bear to face the ship's dinner, I think he put me down as mentally deficient.

I had been in my berth some time before the tremble of

the engines told me that we were off. Determined not to let my nausea keep me in my cabin, as it had done on the outward voyage, I struggled into my clothes each morning and crawled up on deck, so glad to have got past the smell of india-rubber. I made no attempt so much as to look into the dining-saloon. But I had hardly been tucked up in a rug on a deck-chair by kindly fellow passengers before a steward would come along with beef-tea, followed by another with sandwiches. The weather was splendid, and all the other passengers were bursting with health. They were amused at my lying there all day, and used to stop for a chat as they went by, and tease me. 'One would think you were a mamma instead of a girl!' 'If I had to scrub the deck,' I argued, 'I would probably be well enough to do it; but as I have nothing to do, why shouldn't I do as I like?' Concerts and things were going on in the distance, but they couldn't induce me to attend them; so they brought me several books to beguile the time. Of these I tried three: one described a broken-hearted lover, another a forsaken girl, and the third a mother's death-bed. After these I preferred merely revelling in the idea that I was getting nearer England. Lunch-time made a pleasant interlude. A little while before it was due the steward came to me with the menu for me to make a choice, and then the various things were brought to me on a vast tray, served in a most appetizing way. At some time each day the purser sat down for a chat. He was a charming fellow, full of droll anecdotes, and I began to suspect that pursers were chosen simply for their ability to make the voyage agreeable for the passengers.

What with these many chats, the continual little meals, watching men cleaning the already spotless things on the ship, and the excitement of sometimes seeing a steamer in the distance, the days never hung heavily. I compared them with those endless days on the *Adriatic*, and commented on the difference to the purser. 'But they really *are* shorter,' he exclaimed, 'because we are meeting the sun,' and proceeded to explain it at great length. I agreed to all he said very heartily, for I felt I would rather go west again than be made to understand what happened. 'The upshot of it seems to be,' said I, 'that you lengthen your life by travelling west, and if you kept at it thoroughly there is no reason why you should ever die.' He said there was something in my point, but it obviously set him back a pace, and the subject was fortunately dropped.

On the last evening a specially good dinner was laid out on my tray, with real grapes, so different from those I had eaten in America, which looked and tasted as if they had come off a woman's hat. When I remarked on this to the steward he said, 'Captain's dinner—special.' Whether it was the captain's dinner or a rumour flying round that the Scilly Lights were in view, I can't say, but suddenly my legs returned, my head was no longer giddy, and I ran along the deck waving my arm and crying, 'Hurrah for Cornwall'. To think that Tony and Reska-dinnick were just over there! I could hardly sleep that night for excitement, found none of the former difficulty in dressing in the morning, and was early up on deck. I caused a small sensa-tion by going into the dining-saloon for breakfast and eating heartily. 'Whom have we here? A stowaway?' was among the bantering remarks.

Then followed a cheery bustle of good-byes and hopings to meet again, of handing out of letters and sending off tele-grams. For me there was a long letter from Arthur, begging me to give Cornwall the go-by and come straight on to Wales. Instructions were given about distinguishing the various stations at Southampton, about every possible train I might catch, where to change, and how he would expect a telegram as soon as ever I could give particulars. He would come to Southampton to meet me were it not for the old *res angusta*. In case the letter should go astray the more intimate parts were in Welsh and Latin.

I parted regretfully from my friend the deck-steward. Not knowing what was the correct tip, since no one had been waited on as I had been, I confided to him my difficulty, and offered him all the American notes that remained to me. He demurred to this and asked did I know how much it was. I said no, I wasn't at all clear, but it didn't matter, as I was never likely to go to America again.

I had jumped with glee from the gangway and was looking around in sheer delight at being on English ground again, when an elderly man and a younger one approached me, asked me where I was intending to go and what my luggage was, and offered to arrange everything for me, trains and all. While I was explaining Arthur's directions to the older man the younger one had gone off and soon drove up in an open fly with my trunk aboard. He then took me to the right station for Wales, sent my telegram for me, and saw me off. He refused all payment for fly and telegram, and said it was a pleasure. I like to think that these kindly people were not members of some Society for the Protection of Young Females, but were just being helpful to any one bewildered on arrival at a big port.

My train was a rackety old thing, finishing an honourable life no doubt on an unfrequented line. It was one of those soft September mornings when the sleepy country-side looks its best—green fields with overgrown hedges, where the children gathering blackberries stopped to wave at the train . . . old red farms and grey churches. It all reminded me of my mother's saying that England always seemed to her like a garden when she returned from abroad. As we drew near to Winchester I hung out of the window to catch a glimpse of the ancient royal city and the cathedral. In the station the guard strolled up for a word and told me that I was the only passenger. When I said that I had been over to Chicago he was greatly interested, for his wife had a nephew out in those parts, and he felt sure that I must have come across him.

I passed through bits of England that day that I shall probably never see again, for it was an oddly cross-country journey. My first change was at Oxford, where I saw a woman struggling with a child and a lot of luggage. As I helped her along I asked her where she was going. 'Quebec,' said she, 'a terrible long way.' 'It will soon be over,' said I, 'and when you get there it is such a lovely place, something like England, you know. I've just come from there, and I was so sorry to leave it.' This cheered her, and I was able to pack her comfortably in her train before mine came in.

The usual confusion at Shrewsbury seemed quite homely, and the hills of Wales homelier still, and as we slowed down for Machynlleth I saw Arthur at the extreme edge of the platform.

VII

Peter, Martin, and Jack Work Together

§ 1

WHEN work began again in the autumn I felt much richer for my time in America. Not from the speeches at the Chicago Conference, which had made only the slightest impression, but from the mixing with all sorts of people, and seeing how English ways looked from a distance. High-sounding educational theories made a stir and faded out. Ingenious methods took on the same ridiculous aspect as cure-all patent medicines. The only things of permanent importance to a teacher seemed to be to get hold of her pupils' point of view, and work somehow from that. This I knew meant nimbleness of mind rather than long experience; in fact I had observed that long experience, of itself, was often a drawback; your experienced teacher, especially if 'successful', was sure to meet any fresh idea with 'Well, *I* always make them . . .'

What, then, could I do to help these students of mine to a quicker means of getting *en rapport* with their classes? The natural way was to attend their lessons and discuss these afterwards. But the practice we managed to get in the schools was so deplorably little. And sometimes I hardly wondered at this, for despite all our care we had some humiliating experiences. Although the students were all women with diplomas and were assumed to be well educated, reliance could not be placed on their general knowledge. I impressed on them continually that they must not be afraid of questions, that every question from a pupil was a feather in one's cap, and that the ideal lesson would consist entirely of answers to such questions. In accordance with this idea I tried to foresee any likely questions and make sure that the student could answer them. One of our number, a London B.A., was so limited in her range that I used to go over her notes with great care, however simple the subject, lest she should be landed in some awkward hole. In a lesson on the camel, for instance, she had a note to the effect that it could go without food for a considerable time by obtaining sustenance from its hump. This sounded bookish. 'Now suppose,' said I, 'that the class should ask you how the camel does this. What will you say?' As she looked nonplussed, I added, 'Do you think it stretches its head round and takes a bite for lunch?' 'Yes, I suppose it does.' Again, in a lesson on Australia she referred to the penal settlement. 'Now,' said I, 'if a child should ask you where our convicts are sent nowadays, I hope you know?' 'They are sent to Siberia, aren't they?' she replied. The word *portcullis* occurred in some poem she was to teach, and I asked her to draw it, or at least to describe it. No reply. 'Well, do you think it is a kind of Russian soldier?' She thought it probably was. However, ignorance never mattered much so long as they didn't haver and muddle and pretend to know what they didn't. Even specialists can be gravelled in their own subject, but it's quite easy to find things out. In fact, elder pupils can be given books of reference and dig for themselves.

Whatever preliminary pains I took, blush-making mistakes would be made either from ignorance or nervousness, and I used to amuse Arthur with them at the week-end. He said it must be as bad for me to sit and endure blunders and good chances thrown away, as it is for a Junior to watch his Leader ruining his case. 'I am more exhausted by the agony of hearing him spoil point after point than by any amount of work of my own, even bad work of my own.'

My worst experience in this line happened at the school for daughters of the clergy, where I had obtained by means of great meekness and cajolery permission to give a course of lessons. I had at the time a student rather older than the rest, a woman of intelligence and wide culture, who had travelled in Italy and enjoyed the pictures that I had always longed to see. When I suggested that she should give one or two lessons on Italian artists to these daughters of the clergy, she grew quite enthusiastic and prepared notes on Botticelli full of interesting matter and illustrated by good reproductions. The girls, an elder class, were assembled, and I looked forward to a pleasant half-hour, as the student took up her position at the desk and disposed all her illustrations conveniently to hand. But not a word did she utter. Minutes passed. Still not a syllable . . . nor sign . . . nor groan. She didn't look ill. I almost wished she did. The girls began to look at one another and fidget. It seemed much longer, but I suppose it was only ten minutes that we sat expecting her to begin every moment. Then it dawned on me that she had been literally struck dumb with nervousness. I had seen it take very odd shapes, but never such abject paralysis as this. Making some excuse I led her out, and returned to give some kind of a lesson on Botticelli. The girls guessed what was the matter, I think, for they behaved splendidly, as young people always will if things go wrong.

But news of the incident reached the headmistress, who came to me when I was putting on my hat to request that we would not come again. When I pleaded nervousness she replied, 'But you mustn't *allow* them to be nervous.' I am sure she meant this kindly, and she added, what was of course true, that she couldn't afford to have the girls' time wasted like that. So bang went the bit of practice that had been so hard won.

It was no use to blame the poor student, whose contrition, like her feeling for Botticelli, was past words. But we all tried to analyse the malady, and came to the conclusion that the chief ingredients of nervousness were conceit and want of breath. If you don't mind making a fool of yourself (which you are sure to do anyhow) and take a deep breath, you will be able to face anything. It had been the fear of saying something inadequate about Botticelli, conceit in short, that had led to the present distress. The old slogan, 'It is better to remain silent and be thought a fool than to open your mouth and remove all doubt', may be excellent in society, but is no good in front of a class of girls. I cheered them with the reflection that all eminent speakers are nervous on beginning their speeches, however experienced they may be, for Arthur had told me that this was the case with even the best men at the Bar. He said that even an after-dinner speech was not worth anything unless the speaker felt nervous when he started. Realizing that the sky hadn't fallen, the student recovered her poise and was never 'dumb before a Botticelli' again.

Another student was at the opposite pole, giving no trouble to herself or the school, free from nervousness, completely self-confident and humdrum. Of her I despaired, feeling sure that in mature age she would be precisely the same and would retire deeply respected.

Self-confidence, however, could appear in a different and highly interesting form. One student was a specialist in history, had been excited by Mr. Allen's scientific view of it, and was brimful of the notion that a class *must* catch her own spirit of enthusiasm for the subject. Now it chanced that her lot fell to take a class of elder girls in the Marylebone Higher Grade School. Such a tough set they were that the students used to call them 'the lions' den', and suffered tortures of nervousness before facing them. Well, she was for capturing their minds by taking broad sweeps of history, showing them the process of human development through the ages, giving them a graphic idea of the Flow of Time. Standing at a table in front of the 'lions' she opened ostentatiously a very large volume of history, and tossing its pages carelessly to and fro she began brightly: 'To-day we are going to take some event in history, and see what led up to it, and then what flowed from it. Now, girls, tell me any *one* historical fact, in *any* age.' A long pause followed, as may be well imagined, and I sat expectant, incapable myself of thinking of any event at all. At last one of the lions put up a paw. 'Please, Miss, Henry VIII had six wives.' The giggle round the class that followed put the poor student completely off her stroke, and the lesson went to pieces. But she herself had sufficient humour to learn a lesson from her failure. In fact we all profited by it, for I took the occasion to point out (much to the general comfort) the danger of being 'brilliant', of just enjoying oneself and regarding the pupils as an audience. 'Ask yourself,' I said, 'after an apparently successful lesson, whether you have been teaching, or merely performing in front of the class.'

A quite peculiar problem was provided by another student. For some reason or other she had come on to me for a last term after having attended another training college for two terms. All my efforts had to be expended on untraining her. She had learnt to do all the correct things with a precise and devastating thoroughness. Such pains did she take to avoid mistakes in method that her lessons were drained of all spontaneity and were as dull and predictable as an old-fashioned sermon. Every lesson was furnished with a proper introduction, and ended with a summary; the life of a man always began with the Influence of his Times on Him and ended with His Influence on his Times. And yet in ordinary life this girl was sensible and natural. I then saw why so many people objected to training, without being able to say exactly what was the matter with it. I felt that if I could only smash something inside her she would come out well. I put the case before Arthur.

'You say that she does nothing wrong, and yet nothing worth doing?' said he. 'Has she any sense of humour?'

'Oh, plenty, when she isn't teaching; and she has brains.'

'Then why not take the bull by the horns and tell her the story of the man buying a horse at the fair?'

The story ran thus: A man saw a horse that greatly took his fancy—good appearance and every point correct. But the price was absurdly low. He asked what was the matter with it. Did it jib? No. Did it kick? No. Some ugly trick, surely? No, nothing wrong at all. So he bought it, and as soon as the money had been passed over he said, 'Now tell me, what *is* the matter with it?' The former owner replied, 'There's nothing the matter with it, but the horse isn't worth a damn.'

Following counsel's advice I took the bull by the horns, told the story, and got in response a hearty laugh from the student. She was then ready to see that a teacher, too, might be faultless and worthless. 'Cast all methods to the winds,' I suggested, 'and be your natural self. Keep your eye on the class more than on your prepared ideas, be ready for any emergency or change of mood, and like a good horse be able to go the pace.'

It was for this general loosening-up of the minds of the students that we needed more practice so badly. And we suffered not only in the small quantity of teaching allowed us but also in its quality. We were asked to give lessons on subjects that the children already knew well (in which we could do little harm) or else on subjects that were dull, difficult, or unpleasant to take; for instance, a lesson on the plagues of Egypt, and another on Gehazi and Ananias (presumably to teach the dangers of untruthfulness). An example of the too familiar was a lesson on the well-worn Clive, and I was really sorry for the student who had to take it, for she was the one who had endured the anecdote of the horse. But she smiled on me cheerfully as she began. Finding, as we suspected, that the class knew all about Clive's naughtiness as a boy, and also all about the Black Hole, even to the exact number who crawled out alive in the morning, she said, 'Ah yes, I was sure you would know that. But have you ever thought what became of those twenty-three? Their health was undermined perhaps, and they died soon after? Very likely most of them did. But the other day, as I was walking through old St. Pancras churchyard, what should I see but a tombstone to the memory of one of those twenty-three survivors. He had lived to a great age, and I wondered how often he had told the story of that night.' This little atom of reality brought the class to life. Then she suggested that they might act a scene about it : one could be the old man telling the story, the others acting as his grandchildren asking him questions as to who ordered the black hole, and why, who punished him, and how, and any other questions they liked. 'If grandpapa doesn't know something he is asked, it is because his memory is failing with age, and one of the others can say she knows it from hearing him tell it so often before.' The scene went with a swing, and the time was up all too soon. As we left the school I said to her in mock concern, 'You have entirely neglected Clive's Influence on his Times.' 'Yes, thank goodness,' was her happy reply.

In such wrestling with trouble, and building bethels out of stony griefs, the students made the best of bad jobs. Then it occurred to me that I might supplement the meagre school practice by some exercises in College. So I set apart Saturday morning for doing all sorts of things that would help them to get rid of nervousness, to become ready-witted for emergencies, to feel confidence in being able to manage some devices rapidly and well. Sometimes I gave out a subject to be prepared, sometimes the exercise had to be done impromptu. Each student in turn had to tell an anecdote, describe some place, sketch a character from history, or explain something from her special subject (or even stand questioning on it). Sometimes there was a competition in writing on the blackboard, for rapidity and legibility at a distance; or working out a long sum, or arranging heads effectively. Reading aloud, getting variety into the voice, arranging for the others to act a scene, dictating a passage—I thought up all the tortures I could, and at first they were unpopular. But I took care that all criticism should be light-hearted, I thanked those who made fools of themselves for the public good, and in this spirit Saturday mornings became a pleasure for us all.

An exercise in drawing was always part of the programme, and here there was a great deal of recalcitrance to be fought. From America I had learnt the phrase 'talking with the chalk', and I urged the students to throw a little plan or sketch or map on the board to illustrate anything they were explaining or describing. 'It may not be really needed to make the point clear, but it focuses attention if nothing else.' 'Oh, I never could draw,' was of course a common reason for never trying, until I hit on the slogan, 'The worse you draw the better.' I pointed out, what they already knew, that elaborate drawings on the board, so often seen in schools, were a waste of time and ministered only to the vanity of the teacher. 'Draw worse than you really can,' said I, 'and if a pupil looks supercilious invite her to come out and make a better sketch for you. She very likely can, you thank her, and every one is pleased. Poor drawing in the teacher encourages all to have a try, while

perfect drawing has a precisely opposite effect. Welcome every
kind of superiority in your pupils (of knowledge or skill), for
after all they *must* outshine you eventually if you teach well.
Tell them so. Glory in it.' I had got this idea from Rousseau,
the only valuable notion I remember from *Émile*. As for maps,
I insisted that they ought to be able to draw a rough map of
any country from memory, and its position among other
countries; and I waged warfare against the over-elaborated
ones with blue edges and feather mountains that are still
marked 'very good' in school exercise-books.

Short stories and anecdotes were also practised every week,
because there was no knowing when they would come in
useful. Is the weather very hot or very cold? Is some little
disciplinary trouble threatening? Are you attacked (as every
one is at times) by complete blankness about the matter in
hand? You have merely to say 'That reminds me,' and plunge
into a story. The magic words 'once upon a time' will hold
young people back from any dark design, and they will never
worry as to what reminded you. It is interesting to note the
words 'There was a certain man' coming again and again in
the Gospel record. Perhaps the multitude sometimes needed
handling. The mere fact of having a story up your sleeve is
sufficient to impart peace of mind and thus often obviate the
necessity for using it. 'Up your sleeve' can be almost literal if
you make a list of available stories, or sources of stories (such
as Greek and Roman legends, history, Hans Andersen, Grimm,
Norsk and Celtic tales), and keep it in your desk.

These exercises had their use for general class teaching, but
they left untouched the problem of getting at the minds of
individual pupils. 'It's easy,' I said, 'to give a successful lesson
with the aid of a few bright girls, but what about back-row
boredom?' What about those lumpy girls, those White Queens,
who sit in their thousands in English schools, while 'interesting'
lessons are poured over them? In old days they would have
been useful at home, cooking and washing and sewing and
picking up wisdom of a kind. Now the schools are making
them stupid. Every efficient lesson that leaves them untouched

does them harm; they become more dazed, more stupid, less interested in anything at all, and finally manage to marry men who commit suicide.

Each student agreed to select one pupil suspected of such tendency from the schools we attended, and watch her from the back; have a look at her note-book if possible; ask her sometimes at the end of a lesson what she had learnt from it. The reports brought to College were illuminating enough, often depressingly so. Special efforts were made to interest these girls in something—anything. One of those under observation sat mentally asleep week after week in an elder class of a private school, and a rivalry arose as to who should get a gleam of intelligence from her. At last, in a geography lesson, some mention was made of cannibals, with explanation of a very slight kind. 'Do they really eat one another?' exclaimed this girl. When she was assured that it was a fact, she sat up, took notice, and never relapsed into her lethargy.

Another plan I devised for making the most of our small practice was this: each student had a 'shadow', a fellow student (chosen by herself) who went to as many of her lessons as possible during the term, watched teacher and class as a whole, gave her all the help she could, told her of little tricks and mannerisms, and discussed the effect of the lessons on the pupils as it appeared to an onlooker. But none of my devices made up for the lack of plenty of practice. Help was at hand, however, from a most unexpected quarter.

§ 2

One morning the College porter came up to say that two gentlemen were downstairs desirous to see me. To my surprise these were two Roman Catholic priests. After apologies for troubling me for the interview, with excessive courtesy and delicately worded questions, mixed with vague statements, they drew from me (what I was in no way anxious to conceal) the fact that Bedford College was entirely undenominational. Yes, indeed, they had heard a rumour to that effect;

strange as it seemed, no statement of creed or faith was required of its students; not even attendance at prayers was required; nor even the formality of special exemption from prayers.

'Quite,' I answered readily, 'for the simple reason that there are no prayers to be excused from. No one prays here at all, let alone requires any one else to do so.'

At this they smiled a little, and so did I, and then they approached their main point. Their teaching sisters were well educated and devoted to their work, but felt the need of understanding its principles and knowing about modern methods. It was hoped soon to start a training college for them in London; indeed they had a prospective head for it. But she herself was vague as to what the work embraced, and would like to go through a course of training—would like, in short, to attend for a year at Bedford College.

'Just to get hold of our ideas, and then carry them out herself afterwards?' said I. They laughed a little uncomfortably at that, but I immediately added that I thought it a capital idea, and should be delighted to help on the good work as much as possible. We parted with great cordiality, and two nuns were entered, and followed by several more from other convents a little later.

It was those first two nuns that made the greatest impression on me, partly because it was the first time I had made the acquaintance of a nun, but still more because they were both remarkable women and have remained my friends for life. The one who was to become herself the Principal of the Convent Training College somewhat alarmed me on her arrival, for she was ten years older than I was, and had far more experience of teaching. 'Mother St. Raphael' in her convent, she was entered at College as Miss Paley. As I was taking her name down I said, 'Are you any . . .?'

'Yes,' she interrupted, 'I'm his granddaughter.' I need not have feared her wealth of experience, for she was quite humble-minded about it, and ever willing to describe the mistakes she had made in her early teaching, for the benefit and encouragement of the others, as well as to provide apt and often humorous illustrations for any principle I put forward. Her much younger 'sister', Angela Bethell (with the equally beautiful religious name of 'Mary of Assisi'), was one of the most charming girls I have ever met, as well as being one of the finest teachers I ever trained. Many years later she succeeded to Miss Paley's work at the Convent Training College, which has now become a widespread and flourishing institution, sending out every year large numbers of trained graduates—whom I like to think of as my grandchildren.

It was not so much the addition to our numbers that I rejoiced in as the addition to our facilities for practice. The Roman Catholic authorities felt grateful to us, I think, for our hearty welcome to the nuns, for they were generous in allowing us to practise in all their schools within reach. This was a great boon, for the classes were large and the pupils behaved well; in this way the students could get experience in class management without being unduly worried by disciplinary troubles at the same time. I had come to the conclusion that too many difficulties at once may easily discourage a beginner, who needs to be broken in gradually. A lions' den is not a favourable milieu for trying out new ideas, and, after all, rough behaviour with a visiting teacher is the fault of the ordinary teacher, rather than the visitor's.

All this increase in our students and in facilities for practising led Miss Penrose, the new Principal of Bedford College, to feel that she ought to pay a call of courtesy at the convent in Cavendish Square. This she did, but told me afterwards that she had been afraid to go alone and had induced some one to face the ordeal with her. I couldn't help amusing Miss Paley with this terrible adventure, but she pretended great disappointment. 'Oh, what fun we missed!' said she. 'If we had only known we could have locked her in the torture-chamber.' She then told me that a visitor once expressed surprise that they had windows in the convent. 'Oh, yes,' she had replied, 'and if we had time we should look out of them.'

Being ignorant of the daily routine of the convent, I said, when Ash Wednesday was looming, 'Would you like the day off, or to come late, for special services or something?' 'Oh thank you, no,' laughed Miss Paley, 'we get through all that kind of thing *long* before College hours. We are up at five every day, you know.' In fact I was astonished how light-heartedly they took everything, even their religious duties. However, a nun from another convent who shortly arrived was of a different kidney. She had been the headmistress of a large school for several years, and was (perhaps in consequence) extremely lugubrious; and her dress of unrelieved black emphasized her woe. But we soon made her as frivolous as ourselves, for she discovered that in order to be impressive there was really no *need* to be dismal.

Among the lectures that I had to administer I came to feel that those on nebulous psychology were not so valuable as those on famous teachers of the past. A knowledge of how Comenius had started a direct method, how Milton had insisted on practical activity in school, how Pestalozzi had managed to teach single-handed in a barn some fifty young people of all ages, and so on—such knowledge would bring a balanced judgement when the students were later on to be confronted with some world-shaking 'new method'. Now when my syllabus warned me that a lecture on the Jesuits was due, I felt some misgiving. Much as I admired their genius for teaching, I feared that I might say something that was inaccurate or needlessly derogatory to them, while Miss Paley would be sitting there always polite and taking notes, but possibly thinking. So I took her aside a fortnight beforehand, told her plainly my trouble, and suggested that she herself should give the lecture, 'as practice for the future', I urged. To my relief she leapt at the idea, and said she could get the very best material for it from a Jesuit Father to whom she could apply. It was a great success all round, for the other students felt that they were getting the information straight from the horse's mouth, took copious notes, and asked questions which Miss Paley answered ably. In the discussion that followed I raised some points about Jesuit educational methods of which I doubted the wisdom, and all of us, nuns included, were quite outspoken both in approval and disapproval. I had a notion that the nuns enjoyed their perhaps unwonted freedom of speech.

It would be hard to find pleasanter people to deal with than these nuns. My sole objection to them was their habit of wiping their pens on some portion of their voluminous garments. I approached Miss Paley in the matter, but she laughingly replied that its potentiality as a pen-wiper was the main advantage of the get-up.

Looking back on that interview with the priests, I hardly wondered that they had scruples in sending their nuns to us. In those days of definitely denominational institutions, Bedford College was looked upon as godless, indeed almost Unitarian! Perhaps they feared that we might heartlessly persecute any one definitely religious. But as individuals we were all godly enough, and one I remember was fiercely so a Plymouth brother. I should never have discovered her particular shade of belief but for her propensity to preach devastating doctrines in such simple things as a geography lesson. 'This must stop,' I said, 'you may believe that if a good person and a bad person are thrown together the good person is bound to become bad, but I won't have you spreading this gospel among the children.'

As for Roman Catholicism, we others all treated the nuns' faith with courtesy, and they played the game, too, and made no attempts to convert us. The nearest Miss Paley ever came to it was to say one day, 'We shall make a good Catholic of you yet, Miss Thomas.' And when the public examination was impending, and one of the students was dreading failure, a nun pressed an inch-long figure of a saint into her hand and said, 'Take this into the room with you to help you.'

With our numbers going up and examination results good, my salary was raised, I was given an assistant, and Professor Muirhead was appointed to give some very learned lectures on psychology. Sometimes I took a few of the students to an outside lecture, and one of these interested me specially, partly because I knew the lecturer, Graham Wallas, personally, and partly on account of his detached and humorous attitude to education—treated as a rule so absurdly solemnly by lecturers. 'I don't know why I am talking to you about teaching,' said he, 'for I know practically nothing about it. But experience in one walk of life often sheds light on another. Now the subject that I know a lot about is statistics. No connexion with education, you will say at once. But, believe me, statistics can give a wide view of life, and impart great peace of mind, and peace of mind goes a long way in any occupation. For instance, in teaching. Now I hear on quite reliable authority that children in school sometimes misbehave. Let us take the population of England to be forty millions. Tables of statistics will show you exactly what percentage of these millions are attending schools. Well, then, of those attending schools a certain percentage, at any given moment, are bound to be behaving badly. When, therefore, *your* class is behaving badly, say to yourself: "Am I to be exempt from the mathematical law of averages? Am I so marvellous that no child ever misbehaves with me? Am I never to bear my share of the nuisance? What priggishness! What selfishness!" And in the long run, believe me, what a lot of life you would miss.'

VIII

Pisgah

EVERY one has some special place in the world that he wants to see. To-day any one with a holiday and a little money can go almost anywhere, and consequently dashing about has lost much of its zest. But in the nineties it was thought a great thing to go abroad, and any 'travelling' for myself I had placed in some rosy future. Two places had floated in my fancy—America and Italy. I wanted to see the former for its newness and go-ahead ideas, and the latter for its odour of antiquity and its art treasures. As for the equally attractive Greece and Egypt, where parties of people pop about now, they were as remote in my dreams as Tibet. It was annoying to meet people who had the chance to see such places and no power to enjoy them. Just picture my pain in receiving this on a post-card: 'We have been to see the ruins of Carthage; this was a town founded by the Romans in 850 B.C.' My brother Tom had a pupil who was taken to Rome, and on his return asked whether the town he had visited was the *same* as Julius Caesar lived in; he had suspected a kind of fake to attract tourists. He was not a bright boy, for in some public examination he had to 'say what he knew about' various items, among them Flodden. In going over the paper with him afterwards Tom said, 'I suppose you could do Flodden?' 'Oh *yes*, Sir, we spent last summer holidays there!' 'Yes,' said Tom, 'but what happened there?' 'Oh, we just mouched about.'

Well, America had fallen miraculously into my lap, and a year or two later, in a rather absurd way, I was to set foot in Italy. The member of Bedford College Council who had contrived to get me appointed to the training work, and had continued to take interest in all we did, had become very friendly with me in a detached way, and had probably been instrumental in my being selected to go to America. But great was my astonishment at the beginning of a long vacation when she suggested that I should go with her and her sister to Switzerland. I declined, knowing them to be rich people who would travel in a style beyond my means. Since they knew the exact amount of my salary they easily guessed the cause of my refusal, and I was hastily assured that they always went about in the cheapest way they could, and that twelve to fifteen pounds would cover all fares and hotel expenses. I said I would think it over. This meant consulting Arthur (whose existence I kept dark). He had recently been on a trip to Germany with his doctor brother, and got so much interest, chiefly of a political kind, from it that he urged me to take the chance to see something of another country. The chief lack he had felt was some knowledge of German, for ignorance of the language prevented him from hobnobbing with the ordinary people he met —the only real way to get to know a country. Here I felt a bit superior, for hadn't I learnt French from my tenderest years, and French would be all right in Switzerland. So I wrote a note agreeing to go, and was then asked to come for a consultation as to what luggage to take.

The two sisters were the last members of a family to occupy an enormous house at a corner of one of the more dignified of the Bloomsbury squares. I had been invited to dine with them now and again, and had been somewhat overawed by the ritual of the meal. Although they were rigid abstainers, different kinds of wine-glasses were laid for each place. Grace was said, of course, at the beginning, but at a certain moment in the meal a slip cloth was drawn away from the carver's place by a solemn servant and a second grace was said—a mumble that referred, I think, to what we *had* received. I had once been caught by this in the middle of a funny story, and forgot the point. I suppose that this signalized the dessert stage, for elaborate doilies and finger-bowls on fancy plates were brought in, merely for us to look at some oranges and eat two or three grapes. I used to wonder whether all this was a survival of the days when the men were left to their 'walnuts and wine', and, if so, it was easy to see why grace had to be said fairly early. But it was a mystery why such formalities should be retained by two ladies of middle age, teetotallers, with very small appetites. Perhaps it was to pass the time, but more likely it was to keep the servants up to the mark, just as the drawing-room was 'turned out' every Tuesday, however spotless it might be.

The house had been built to last till doomsday; stone stairs were taken up as far as the first floor; steel burglar-proof doors protected the basement with its world of kitchens, pantries, sculleries, and cellars. The furniture was all of the substantial kind now called Victorian and valued as period pieces—huge bookcases, wardrobes, washing-stands, tallboys; but no chairs built for comfort. During the long years of my intimacy with these friends I can recall no change in the position of tables, looking-glasses, settees, and so on, not to mention any variety in the pictures, or vases on the mantelpieces.

The sister with whom I had most to do was the younger one, named Henrietta. I fancy that a boy had been hoped for and the wish had crept into her name, and indeed into her nature, for she was always masterful. After a while I softened her name into Yetta, the Norwegian form of it, dear to me from association with a friend of my mother's called Yetta Barnholt. Henrietta ruled everybody she came across, and if she made an enemy thereby she enjoyed a fight. The lines that Sir Herbert Richmond wrote of Gertrude Bell might well be applied to her:

> *From Trebizond to Tripolis*
> *She rolls the Pashas flat*
> *And tells them what to think of this*
> *And what to think of that.*

She was the master mind in the home régime, and her elder sister, Mary Jane (always clipped to M'Jane), although nominally head of the house, had neither power nor influence. Her duties were confined to sitting at the head of the table, and 'doing' the tradesmen's books. She went into the kitchen every morning to receive instruction from the cook as to what would be best for dinner, and what should be finished up for lunch, what groceries needed replenishing, what linen needed repairing, and so on. She was the more lovable of the two sisters, partly on account of her failings. She would lose bills, write cheques twice, mislay keys. . . . To help her to more business-like habits Yetta presented her with a roll-topped desk, but the multitude of little drawers only meant more places to lose things in, and it was pathetic to see her sitting in front of it disconsolate. Well, you could be sure of her sympathy if you made a mistake or forgot something; in fact she never saw faults in any one.

I knew only a little of the characteristics of these two sisters when I watched their arrangements for Switzerland, and I was amazed. They had been there many times before, and knew exactly what would be wanted to meet every emergency. 'The great point,' said Yetta, 'is to take as small packages and as few things as possible.' This harmonized with my ideas to the full, but their ideas of what was necessary were at the poles from mine. I wish I could remember all the things they had collected for the trip: there were clothes for every caprice of weather; a packet of tea, 'because you can't get drinkable tea abroad'; medicines for every complaint, including the one that my aunt Tony once referred to in a letter thus: 'I am suffering, dear, from what I cannot spell'; rolls of Mead's plaster in case of accidents; soap; biscuits; guide-books; mackintosh squares ('to sit on when we are out'); maps mounted on linen; scissors that folded up; a pocket aneroid ('to see how high we go up the mountain'); Dutch bulb-catalogues; dark glasses to wear in the snow; mending-kit and knitting-wool; two midget packs of cards (they didn't approve of card-playing, but were great at patience, about which they owned a book that detailed sixty-one varieties); unbreakable horn mugs that fitted into one another; elastic bands to gird up their skirts for going up a mountain-side; halma-men and board; a saucepan that served as a tea-kettle and a teapot too, because the tea, enclosed in a muslin bag, could be put in when the water came to the boil. All these things are confused in my memory as they were in the packages, for the only system on which they were put close together was 'fitting in' (such as stockings snuggling round a medicine bottle). I gave great pleasure by my surprise and admiration as each item found its niche, and by exclaiming at the end, 'Why, it has all come out like a game of patience!' The only object I felt unhappy about was the methylated spirit-lamp. I told them of a note I had heard of posted up in a Swiss hotel—'All tin kitchen is defended.' M'Jane laughed softly and said that no one would ever *detect* her in evil-doing, and as time went on I found this to be no empty boast.

The sisters seemed to have all commodities in common; it was only on the intellectual side that the difference between them was glaring. Yetta was remarkably clever at all practical affairs; anything that she organized was sure to be correct to the last button; she always knew exactly what to do, where to go, how to get there, what it would cost, and how long it would take; trains were looked up and rooms engaged ahead. But I never saw her reading anything with interest except a guide-book. M'Jane was at the other extreme, caring nothing for plans, falling in happily with any arrangement, and unobtrusively pursuing her hobbies. Among these was botany, of which she had an extensive knowledge in spite of the fact that her only garden consisted of a few square yards of 'leads', richly endowed with London soot. One of the chief attractions of Switzerland was the chance it gave her for finding plants that she had met with only in her reference books. These were two huge illustrated volumes, strongly bound to stand wear and tear, and heavy with many coloured plates. It was over these that I noticed the first rift between the two sisters. M'Jane gave way to Yetta in nearly everything, but there were one or two points about which she was obstinate (delightfully so, I thought). I saw her firmly placing these books at the bottom of one of the trunks, paying no attention at all to Yetta's look of annoyance and protest of 'Must those heavy things really be taken?' To my amusement they became a permanent cause of unrest and acrimony throughout our trip whenever repacking had to be done.

As a final piece of advice they suggested that I should waterproof my walking skirt, since sudden showers must be expected. This sounded good, and I asked how it was done. 'Quite easy; you take it out of the band, dip it in a gallon of water containing a solution of. . . .' Then followed queer things like gum arabic; but I had lost count after the first sentence, for the very idea of taking a skirt out of its band was enough for me, since I had no notion how to get it in again, and decided to get wet and be done with it. This reminded me of the flask of brandy I forgot to take to America, and I told them that I should be sure to take it in my trunk for Switzerland. They were so shocked that I dropped the subject, fully intending, however, to take it in lieu of waterproofing my skirt.

Yetta undertook to get the tickets and post them to me, and in a few days they arrived in a little green case, with instructions to be at the station on the following Monday morning a little before nine. I spent most of the interval in selecting the rigidly necessary for my small trunk, and then in tidying up my room and destroying old letters in case I died abroad. The really pleasant things to take I left till Arthur came to spend Sunday afternoon with me. We agreed that sketching things were necessary, and at least one book. Keats was the final choice, because I could learn a lot of him by heart. The only thing beside the trunk was a leather satchel that I had bought in Boston, useful for stowing little odd things wanted in train or boat, and for carrying sketching things when we were walking, for it could be slung over my shoulder.

When everything seemed complete Arthur said, 'Now are you absolutely ready for to-morrow morning? Tickets, money, small change?' 'Yes. I've put three fivers in my ticket case, and my purse with small change in my satchel, with a handkerchief and extra scarf. See, here they are.' But there they weren't. All present and correct except the ticket case. I glanced round the room, expecting to see it on the mantelpiece, or some such natural perch. Nowhere. 'I must have packed it by mistake,' said I, and made a few dives into the trunk without result. 'Let's comb the room,' said Arthur, and so we did, even to turning out every drawer. Then in some disgust I turned out all the things in my trunk that had been squeezed in so cunningly. When all were put back we began on the room again, in the unlikely places, behind the chest of drawers, under the rug. 'You might have carried it into the kitchen,' said Arthur, 'let's have a look.' But the bald sink and gas-ring were incapable of harbouring a stowaway. Unfortunately I had no Miss Rogers to call upon for help; she could get any one out of any hole; but she had left, and I was now sharing a flat with a stranger, who was out for the day; and no one had been in to see me and taken the case off by mistake. It looked like one of those murder stories where the corpse is found in a sealed room. But it was no laughing matter. My purse contained nothing more than silver enough for first expenses, and Arthur had only a few shillings in his pocket. Banks were shut, even if I could have afforded to take out any more money. Clearly I should have to give up the trip and send a telegram to Yetta.

We were wondering how best to word this when we heard the key in the door indicating the return of my neighbour. I was so full of spleen that I would have appealed anywhere for help, but expected no more than kind sympathy when I waylaid her in the passage and told her my trouble. 'Let me have a look,' said she cheerfully, 'I have a flair for finding things.' After going over the places we had already searched, she went into the kitchen, at which we couldn't help laughing. 'I noticed that your room was peculiarly tidy,' said this female Sherlock Holmes, 'free from one's usual clutter of papers lying about. Have you been destroying old stuff? Letters and things?' Yes I had, so she suggested the dustbin. We had one of those grey sanitary things, emptied officially daily, and my latest deposit into it had been the vegetable parings and other refuse from lunch. I was disgusted at the idea of unveiling these, but she urged me to leave no potato unturned, and soon I came upon a lot of discarded papers, and amongst them the precious green case. In another few hours it would have been

carried away by the dustman. As soon as Arthur had gone I
went to her room to thank her again, and express admiration
of her acumen. 'I didn't like to tell you in front of Mr.
Hughes, lest he should laugh at me,' said she, 'but I always carry on my
watch-chain this little charm. It's an eye of Horus, very valuable. You can see some just like it in the British Museum.
It was given me by an egyptologist, who told me that the little
god in it would always find anything I lost.'

§ 2

We had not been travelling many hours before I realized
the comfort of being with some one who could arrange
things ahead. There was none of the adventurous freedom
of my time in America, but a foreign country was so new to
me that every object and incident was exciting. Getting
through the customs at Calais—my first experience of French
politesse—disappointing. Buying a brioche at Amiens refreshment room—my first experience of French *cuisine*—celestial.
Our way from Geneva to Chamonix was by diligence, and I
thought of the schoolboy's howler about Caesar contending into
Gaul on the top of a diligence. Never before had I known
what dust and thirst could be. We pulled up half-way at some
hostelry; other passengers were allaying their thirst, and I
boldly ordered a lemonade, thereby shocking M'Jane and
Yetta. They thought it was not the thing to be seen drinking
outside a public house. More the thing, I argued, than to be
seen doing it inside. But they were not amused, and I bore in
mind that any reference to 'drink' was taboo.

In order to give me the best possible holiday Yetta had
picked out all the places, however well known to herself and
her sister, that would interest me most, and be most representative of the scenery, including a few famous spots, and others
less frequented and more 'distinguished'. Our first objective
was Mont Blanc, whose height I had learnt at school, but of
which I knew no more than a fellow pupil who had spelt it
Blanc Mange.

'What war is on?' I asked, as we rattled into Chamonix, for men in uniform were making menacing approaches to our diligence, and I hoped to have fallen in with one of those revolutions always going on in France.

'Those aren't soldiers,' said Yetta, as she singled one out for notice, 'they're hotel attendants. Each one wants to capture a customer for his hotel. Lots of people don't decide their hotel till they get to a place.'

My room was very small, and completely bare of everything but necessities. The wooden floor was pock-marked, the result, so I learnt, of continual wear from climbers' boots. How glad I was of a wash and change from my dusty things, and how hungry I was. To my dismay I heard that instead of being seven o'clock, a natural time for dinner, it was only six o'clock, for we had come out of Switzerland into France, and the times varied. That hour seemed endless; the weather was cloudy, and the outlook from my window reminded me of Wales on a wet day.

Next morning I woke to find the sun streaming in, and jumped up at once to look out of the window. Honestly, I nearly fell down with surprise. There was Mont Blanc, cloudless, dazzling, right against me. The shout I gave brought Yetta to my door. 'Ah, yes,' said she, smiling with pleasure at my excitement, 'I chose that room for you on purpose. My sister and I know the view quite well, and we have said nothing to you about snow mountains so that you might have this surprise. We were so glad that it was cloudy yesterday when we were all so tired. You have got the full beauty just at the right moment. Hope you weren't disturbed by the early starters.'

'I was too fast asleep to be disturbed, but who are they?'

'The people in the hotel who are making for the top to-day. There'll be a gun fired when they reach it. Their progress is watched through that big telescope you see below in the yard.'

'Are *we* going to do any climbing?' I asked, knowing that it was either ordained beforehand, or impossible.

'No, rope-work is too much of a business; we will walk

far up the slopes, though, and we can climb to Montenvers, and cross the glacier.'

I found this kind of expedition quite exciting enough, for Yetta had planned each outing cleverly so that some complete surprise should reward a tough walk, no matter from what centre we started. Once, I remember, we trudged upwards for several hours, to come suddenly upon a ridge with the whole Bernese Oberland stretched in front of us. And our leisurely pace had its advantages, giving M'Jane a chance to botanize and me to make a quick sketch. I was completely satisfied, except within. The mountain air and long walks gave me an outrageous appetite not shared by my companions. Our breakfast consisted of *café complet*. I made it as 'complet' as I could, but was ravenous by midday, when our lunch at some little mountain shanty consisted of *café complet* again. Once, on noticing several people having eggs, I proposed that we should have some too. Yetta thought it rather extravagant, but I shall never forget those glorious *œufs sur le plat* that they served us.

Afternoon tea we used to contrive in our hotel on our return from a long walk. M'Jane engineered it. During breakfast, no matter what the hotel, whether crowded or sparse, she managed to steal several rolls, concealing them in her lap, and taking great pride in the fact that neither Yetta nor I caught her in the act.

In the afternoons, while she was manœuvring her 'tin kitchen' with equal stealthiness, I was dispatched downstairs to procure some milk. The first time I was sent on this errand I thought up a polite way of asking for it in French, using a word for a jug that I had learnt in a 'vocabulary'. The waiter was hopelessly puzzled, and then said, 'If Mademoiselle would speak English!' I did, and received the milk at once. A bit humiliating, considering the large proportion of my life that I had spent in 'learning French'. However, on one occasion I came out strong. An old lady in an hotel wanted a footstool, and none of us could remember the French word for it. 'Leave it to me,' said I, and approaching the proprietor

I said, 'Un petit table pour les pieds, s'il vous plaît.' He nodded and brought one. In fact I could generally manage to scrape together some words that would do to ask the way, the price, the time, or some dire necessity we had forgotten. My trouble began when the natives replied. Here it was Yetta who came in. She couldn't speak French but she had the far rarer gift of being able to understand it; so together we managed quite well, I asking the question, and she standing by to listen for the answer. In remote regions, among the Swiss peasantry, I was helpless. Once we were far away from the hotel up a mountain-side, all set and eager for tea, which we had brought with us, stolen rolls, milk, tin kitchen and all. No, not all. M'Jane had packed the basket and forgotten the matches. Yetta let fly and scolded heartlessly. I couldn't bear it, and offered to explore among the few chalets we had passed *en route*. 'They must have matches,' said I as I started off. No doubt they had, but the word *alumettes* made no impression, nor did any gesture, and I have wondered what one *could* do to express matches. I had to go all the way back to the hotel, and was foolish enough to try a short cut through a lane so deep that it had not enjoyed fresh air for centuries. A cup of tea can be too expensive. If M'Jane herself had struggled in the chalets she would very likely have succeeded, for it was one of the intellectual surprises that she sprung on me that she could carry on animated conversations in patois with our carriage-drivers and other country folk whose talk was Greek to Yetta and me. How had she picked it up? Probably from deep sympathy with their lives, and getting to talk with them 'on the quiet', as she did everything.

The only substantial meal of the day was the dinner in the evening, and even that was not always substantial enough for me; very lengthy and interesting, but I often felt that I could have gone through it all again. The social side was pleasant, for we made friends with our fellow guests, especially when we were in one of those high-up and distinguished hotels where only English people penetrated as a rule. We came across Edmund Gosse complaining of the inferior company at our hotel in Saas-Fee; we met Septimus Buss (a clerical brother of Miss Buss) climbing up the pilgrim path from Saas im Grund; we found Joshua Fitch sitting disconsolate in St.-Luc, as though educational methods had taken all joy from his life. In the high Weisshorn hotel we made friends with a certain Sidney Flemming. 'Do you happen to know a friend of mine called Percy Flemming, the eye-specialist?' said I. 'Not very well,' was the reply, 'he's only my brother.'

There were about a dozen of us at that hotel, all English, and one day the proprietor made a gesture by arranging an all-English dinner. It was a hotter day than usual, quite the last on which to welcome an English dinner. The only course I can now recall was a Christmas pudding, always hateful to me even in my childish days and in the wintry season. The poor man understood that it should be served in flames of brandy, but having no brandy he used methylated spirit, and brought the dish in himself all aglow with pride. Among our company was a well-known artist named Stone, and that heroic man actually ate his portion, saying that he couldn't bear to hurt the feelings of old Mosoni.

In one of our specially English hotels two strangers came in one day, and behaved queerly enough to alarm me. They talked and gesticulated across the table in a violent temper, and I expected that they would come to blows. Yetta laughed at my concern, 'They are only Italians, probably discussing the weather or some travelling difficulty; they never talk quietly.'

That dreaded period of hotel life—the after-dinner stretch of boredom—was not so bad in Switzerland, for we all had plenty to do, and very seldom fell back on halma or patience. Yetta would have maps and guide-books spread about her and be planning our itinerary for the morrow, filling in gaps with knitting. She even taught me to knit. But what I much preferred was to make pencil sketches of the people in the room. Nobody minded this; indeed they all took great interest in being done, and wanted to see the results. M'Jane spent her time mostly in making up the accounts. As the day went on she paid for everything, and then made apparently scrupulous calculations as to how much Yetta and I had to pay her. I thought of how my brothers used to say that on this system it was the man who paid who came off worst. I'm sure that M'Jane forgot much of her outlay. Her next business was to enter in her diary everything that had happened during the day, even vagaries of weather. These duties performed, she then revelled in her hobby, looking up in her botanical books any specimens she had found, and setting aside any worthy ones for her *hortus siccus* at home. Failing any such acquisitions, she would go over her Dutch bulb catalogues, to mark what she would order for the autumn. This I used to call 'M'Jane bulbing'. Meanwhile we chatted freely with our fellow guests, and it was owing to some point being raised by one of them—some doubt as to which of the Queen's children had married whom—that I discovered another of M'Jane's odd accomplishments: she had a complete and reliable knowledge of the Royal Family, and all its relationships, to the remotest cousin. The oddity of this lay in the fact that the sisters, although conservative to the core, were quite militant liberals, following every turn of Gladstone's mind with religious enthusiasm. At least that was true of Yetta. Of M'Jane I had my doubts, guessing that she had secret leanings towards more colourful politics and even towards the Church.

On Sundays we used to take a walk of no great length, giving a rest to sight-seeing, sketching, and botany, and sitting about to read. It was thus that I caught M'Jane with another book that she had privily packed—a selection of rather unusually deep religious *pensées* and poems. When I showed great interest in these she said, 'I keep this in the background, dear, as my sister does not care for it. She has been embittered about all kinds of religion. You see, we are Unitarians, and are looked upon as atheists, and by many people as inferior socially.' That seemed to me an absurd idea, and as soon as occasion offered I asked Yetta what the Unitarian creed was that it should be thought so disgraceful. The answer came out as pat as from a penny in the slot: 'We believe in the father-hood of God, and the brother-hood of man.' 'But surely,' said I, 'that's just what Church people believe, and can't be offensive to any one?' She shrugged her shoulders and spread out her hands, and then added a definition of the sect that evidently pleased her greatly. It was the remark made by a business man who had been asked what Unitarians believe: 'I don't know what they believe; all I know about them is that they pay twenty shillings in the pound.'

Her scrupulous honesty about money amounted to a religion in itself, a kind of odd mammon-worship. A penny was a sacred thing, never to be treated lightly, as in the phrase 'It's only a penny'. She had a slogan, 'Never lend more money than you can afford to lose'. Clothes and household goods were never to be given away unless they were clearly of no more use. M'Jane was far looser in her morals. She used to give away things surreptitiously to the undeserving, and try to look innocent when the inevitable question arose, '*What* has become of that spare strip of carpet?'

Yetta's animosity to the Church was aggravated by the behaviour of the usual visitors in the hotel. On Sunday morning they would turn the dining-room into a temporary church, and have the Anglican service performed by any clergyman who happened to be on holiday. All well and good, but the fuss in clearing the room, arranging seats, setting out flowers, and expecting silence in the hotel, was annoying to those who belonged to another communion and distasteful to many ordinary Church people. While Yetta remained rather snortingly aloof, M'Jane and I would sometimes go in search of any native gathering we could find. Once we enjoyed an ancient ritual to celebrate some saint. On the pilgrim path from Saas im Grund up to Saas-Fee there were a number of little chapels of a fascinating kind, and it was in the largest of these that we joined a congregation of peasants dressed in their gayest clothes, marching, singing, and carrying banners, and M'Jane understood some of what they were praying and singing about.

When we were in Berne we induced Yetta to go with us to

the cathedral, since the Lutheran service was bound to be fairly Protestant. Protestant it obviously was, for anything less like a Roman Catholic ritual it would be hard to imagine. Not a word could I understand, and had to deduce from the parson's manner in the pulpit (where he remained all the time) whether he was reading the Bible or preaching or praying. I got no hints from the attitude of the congregations, for they sat through everything, even when singing a hymn. At least I suppose it was a hymn, but the only sound was a kind of hum, given forth in a rhythmic swing mildly suggestive of a tune. Suddenly M'Jane passed urgent word along the pew that we were to go out. She was so seldom imperative in her mood that we knew it was not to be questioned, and sidled out at once, fearing she was ill. But when we got into the open air she seemed quite herself, and Yetta asked her what on earth she had ordered us out for. 'I saw Molly's face,' said she, 'and felt sure that one of her sudden bursts of laughter was imminent.'

§ 3

To those who know Switzerland it would be useless to name the centres we visited, and tedious to those who don't know it. I will only mention a few, just to give an idea of the trouble Yetta must have taken to plan a holiday that would give me an all-round idea of the country. We drove along the Rhône valley to the hotel at its head, and thence we climbed up by the side of the glacier to the St. Gothard Pass. We went by the rack-and-pinion railway to the Rochers de Naye. We cruised on Lake Geneva, and visited the Castle of Chillon. We had the exciting but rather fearful experience of groping along the wooden track through the Aarschlucht. And, far more delightful than any of these, we found remote places where we could gather the small blue gentian, *Linnaea borealis*, and even the very rare edelweiss.

We were at Saas-Fee one evening, at our usual after-dinner occupations, when I joined Yetta in her itinerary work for the next day. We had her big map spread out on the floor, showing the mountain-ranges all grey and forbidding. 'How near we seem to Italy,' I muttered, thinking that perhaps one day Arthur and I might be rich enough to go there together. 'Let's go there to-morrow,' said Yetta quite quietly, without looking up, and running her finger along the map. 'We could do it from here, but it means a long walk, too far for M'Jane.' She was within earshot and immediately said, 'You two go; I shall be so glad of a day to myself here, to look up lots of flowers in my books.' Whereupon we seized maps and guide-books with fresh energy, and saw that we could reach the Monte Moro Pass if we put up somewhere for a night on the way, and then we could get back by the following night. 'The view from the summit is grand in the extreme,' I read aloud from the guide-book, and added, 'I could have told the author that.' Yetta was looking pessimistically for a possible place to spend the night. 'There's something they call an inn,' said she, 'but they say no more at all; goodness knows what it will be like.' 'But an inn is an inn,' said I, 'it must be able to take us *in*, and what more do we want?'

We were to be off by 6.30, and Yetta warned me to go as light as possible, taking nothing in my satchel but the barest needs for the night. Keats must stay behind then, but I couldn't go to Italy without taking some treasure to share it with me. Now I had got in my trunk a very small prayer-book that I never needed but kept by me for its association with my father. He had given it to me when I was four years old—a lovely little volume, bound in leather with a gilt clasp, and bright rubrics that cheered me through the litany. When I could read I thought it would be nice to follow what they were saying in my book, so one Sunday morning I took it to my brother, 'Tell me, Tom, how far they've got in this book. I want to begin reading it to-day in church.' 'Here you are,' said he, pointing to 'The wicked man'. 'How funny,' said I, 'that they should be starting to-day, just when *I* want to start!' 'They start there every time,' said Tom. I gasped, 'What! this whole book every time!' 'Yes, more or less,' said he, and I put off my scheme to a future date. In fact the print was too small for easy use, but the little book was a constant companion, and I tucked it into my satchel for Italy.

Our route was unfrequented by tourists, and passed many little villages, each with its cupola-topped church tower, and sketchable bits everywhere, and the weather superb. I can't remember what we did for lunch, but I know that we arrived very tired and hungry at the 'Mattmark See Hotel'. I have stayed at many queer hostelries in my time, but none quite so outlandish as that. We were too hungry to be critical of the supper, and too tired to do more than have a look at the lake— a dreary affair—before we felt inclined for bed. There was only one bedroom to be had, and this was only large enough to hold two little beds and a minute washing-stand furnished with a basin no bigger than a pudding-bowl and a jug of water to correspond, and one small towel. But there was no lack of moisture in the beds. Yetta, who was a folio edition of a woman, could hardly get into hers, and I spent much of the night bunching myself up so as to get as little of the damp as possible. 'It's a good thing,' said I, 'that we are to be called at four; we shan't have to be in these beds for long.' The early start was necessary, not only that we might get back to Saas by nightfall, but also that we might see the sunrise effects. Provided with some stale rolls by the inn (I guessed that bread was brought to them once a fortnight, and that we were near the end of a batch) for our lunch on the way, we started off along the roughest and stiffest road I have ever known. But what mattered the road, what mattered a poor night and a vile breakfast, what mattered anything at all, when one was so blessed as to be able to see the glow on the mountains before the sun rose? No sunset can equal it, nothing on earth can equal it. I think Beethoven must have had such a scene in his mind when he composed the andante movement of his Fifth Symphony.

We reached the top of the pass about midday, and allowed ourselves half an hour for seeing Italy. As we were struggling up I had at the back of my mind the blue distances in Titian's pictures, and now I saw what he had seen. I sat down in Italy and champed my stale roll in a vast contentment. Thoughts of the great painters, thoughts of Hannibal, scraps of Roman history crowded into my mind, but the dominating interest was the knowledge that it was Virgil's country, and taking out my little prayer-book I wrote in it 'Italy', then the date, and then a favourite phrase from the *Aeneid*.

Whenever I am asked if I have visited Italy, I reply 'Yes,' and if the inquirer is sufficiently interested (very rare) to ask my impressions of it my reply is ready: 'I found the scenery magnificent; but I didn't think much of the food I had there.' People are usually too anxious to give their own impressions, and to recommend good hotels, to pursue their inquiries further.

I have never paid a proper visit to Italy, nor indeed have I ever been on the Continent at all since those jolly holidays over forty years ago. No doubt there have been vast improvements in travelling since then. But comfort and convenience deprive one of a lot of fun. One incident on our return journey gives me a pleasanter memory than a great deal of smooth travelling in later days on our own railways. At Dijon we had a stop of twenty minutes at about seven o'clock in the evening. The station restaurant was well prepared for the usual invasion of about fifty passengers, all seizing their only chance of dinner. We were swiftly ushered to our seats at long tables, and immediately waiters bore down upon us carrying our first course. Each waiter carried six plates of hot soup extended on his left arm, and dispensed them to us with his right, exhibiting such extraordinary skill that not a drop was spilt. No sooner was the soup delivered than each waiter dashed away and reappeared with plates of fish to be doled out in like manner. Course followed course, and plates were snatched away, till we reached the cheese. At this stage alms-boxes were handed round, into which we dropped our money, and then rushed to the platform where the train was panting for the start. I remember falling head-long on to the floor of the carriage, overcome with laughter. 'Do try not to laugh, dear,' said M'Jane; 'after that dinner, it may make you ill.'

IX

Preparations

§ 1

THE year 1896 was humming with preparations for the Queen's coming Jubilee. Arthur and I too were humming a little on our own account. The Golden Jubilee had been the occasion of our first meeting, and we thought it a good idea to be married in the Diamond one. The risk was great, but the future was bound to be uncertain, wait we never so long. Arthur had built up a fair practice at the Bar, and I had saved a nest-egg of two hundred pounds, so, we thought, why not? and fixed on 1897 as our second lucky year. Realizing that I should have no more chance, when married, of paying 'bachelor' visits to my brothers, I determined to allot my remaining holidays between them—Christmas with Tom and Easter with Dym. A third visit, an earlier summer one, was thrown in, and it so chanced that these three visits served as a preparation for married life, since they gave me a glimpse of it in three important stages—in the second year, in the tenth year, and in middle age. The visits came in the reverse order chronologically, and that is the order I must follow.

It was in the summer that a barrister friend of Arthur's, named James Corner, invited us both to spend a fortnight at his place in Hereford. Holmer Park was a real 'place' in the old-fashioned sense—a mansion in large rambling grounds, with horses and carriages, friendly dogs, and other animals everywhere about. There must be hundreds of such places in England, and I should not mention our visit were it not for the unusual characteristics of the owners. Mr. and Mrs. Corner were rich and contented. Their one son was now grown up, and they were left alone to enjoy together a delightful middle age. I have come across a few wealthy people and an untold number of jolly people, but this combination of wealth, jollity, and middle age is unique in my experience. The servants of the establishment seemed endless—maids, grooms, gardeners, and odd boys about, all busy over something. But it was Mrs. Corner herself who opened the door to us when we drove up from the station; and although we had resplendent meals, there was none of the fussy formality of being over-waited upon that detracts from the fun.

We were taken for long drives in the country, shown the cathedral and other interests of the town, including the old house that had once been the Butchers' Guildhall. Here the carvings amused us, for the sainted bullocks with wings and what looked like haloes gave the impression of the beasts in Revelation. We had lazy afternoons pottering in the garden, the stables, the kennels, and the poultry-runs, or lying in hammocks and reading. New books and periodicals were scattered about untidily everywhere, competing with the dogs for the best chairs. In short, it was a house to delight a man, being at once comfortable and well mauled.

But it was the talk that I enjoyed most. I never can see why 'shop' should be considered boring. I wanted nothing more entertaining than to hear Mr. Corner and Arthur discussing their cases and the clever advocacy of Carson and other legal stars of the day. I would hear tantalizing scraps like this: 'My case was quite hopeless, but I saw my little jury.' 'The judge was hesitating . . . he might come down on either side . . . so I gave him a cushion to sit on—a little case on all fours with ours—and he sat.' Both Mrs. Corner and I were pleased with one of her husband's stories, because it showed how a woman could outwit men: this female criminal had to be conducted by train to prison in the charge of two police-officers. At a junction there was a change and a short wait, she demanded to be released in order to visit the ladies' room; the two men kept guard outside the waiting-room door; time passed, and they grew anxious about catching their train; on investigation they found that the inner room was connected with the first-class one, and their prisoner had merely walked quietly through and was well away.

When Mrs. Corner and I were alone we had many pleasant talks. She had no pretentions to learning or wide reading, but she had acquired a philosophy of life that filtered through to me as she talked. It might have sounded mere commonplace had it not been illustrated every hour of the day by her own life; and later on I learnt that she and her husband had had their full share of trouble. 'I'm old enough to give you some advice on married life, dear,' said she, 'and, believe me, to be really happily married is a work of art, just like a painting or a piece of music, and I think myself that it's the greatest of all. Don't be surprised if there are dark shadows too. Surely life without any griefs or worries would be as fatiguing as if there were nothing else, and certainly dull.'

'What do you think,' said I, 'of Dr. Johnson's remark when he heard that a married couple had never had a quarrel— "What a damned dull life they must have had!"?'

'Did he say that? Then I don't think much of his wisdom.'

'I'm so glad you feel like that,' said I, 'for it has always seemed to me neither funny nor true.'

'The wonder to me,' said Mrs. Corner, 'is that any one thought it worth preserving. I suppose the old fellow was thinking of those humdrum couples who seem to live like vegetables with no spirit even to be annoyed.'

Encouraged by her views on this subject I then asked her opinion of another thing that had troubled me a little. An uncle's kindly advice had been, 'Be sure you don't expect too much of one another.' This seemed to me such a half-hearted insipid way of starting a great adventure. 'Yes, yes,' broke in Mrs. Corner eagerly, 'fancy being cautious all the time, afraid to ask, afraid to give, lest you should be asking too much or giving too much! No, dear, just go headlong at things together, and life will get more splendid as time goes on.'

§ 2

The visit to my brother Tom in the Christmas holidays of '96 showed me married life at a mid-way stage, and in circumstances unlike that of the Corners. Tom was classics master in the High School at Middlesbrough, and lived in a small house in the town with his wife and two boys aged nine and eight. Naturally economy was necessary, but Nell had brought it to a fine art and obviously enjoyed it. This suited my tastes, and one year we had had a race to see which should spend less on clothes. 'Mind, Molly,' said Nell, 'you've got to put down every penny you spend, if it's only a bit of boot-mending.' The fact that she actually won this race throws a light on her character, for I was near the limit in doing without. Another trait we had in common was the love of little unnecessary expenditures, such as morning coffee at Amos Hinton's when we were shopping. And we never went for a country walk with the little boys without a packet of sweets. Nell used to excuse herself for this by saying, 'Sweets adds'—a phrase made more convincing by its oddity of grammar.

Nell and I together tried all sorts of cooking dodges. Her main cookery book was one issued by some meat-extract company. 'They are splendid recipes,' she explained, 'if you do all they say and just leave out the meat-extract.' Susan, the little daily maid, fetched and carried, stared and laughed, and I am sure hoped for failures, for these she was allowed to carry home, where her young brother, she assured us, was in bed, in a creditable condition.

My term had ended earlier than the school terms, so that I arrived some ten days before Christmas. This provided me with another preparation for married life. On the morning after my arrival the two little boys, Viv and Llew, showed me with great pride the copy-books they had been doing: 'Auntie is coming' was displayed a dozen times in large round hand. While I was loudly admiring these Nell broke her scheme to me: would I be a brick and give them a short lesson in arithmetic every morning?

I was glad that we were allowed to use Tom's study for these lessons, for no one could have done arithmetic in the drawing-room. Here Nell had carried out the vogue of the day. The fireplace was draped with art serge and muslin to represent a spider's web, with a huge imitation spider involved in it. Bulrushes stood in a big jar, wooden stools had red satin ribbon tied round them, and a mirror on the wall had water-lilies painted on it. I shouldn't remember these items so well (for the family naturally avoided the room) had it not been for the piano, on which I practised every day.

Nell had timed things well. The boys were 'just about to begin division', she told me brightly. Now Mr. Harding had made a great point of keeping clear for children the two meanings of division. But I flung these to the wind, and fell back on the 'Nines into eight won't go' method. Each side of me sat an eager little nephew. On my right Viv forged ahead, but on my left Llew hung back and pleaded his youth: 'I think I am too small for division, Auntie.' Now Nell had warned me that this kind of thing might happen, but that Llew was quite as capable as Viv. So I agreed heartily, 'Quite right, darling, you are far too little for division. You shall do a nice long addition while Viv and I are busy.' So saying I set him an easy and laborious sum. After a bit I sensed that the eyes on my left were wandering towards the problem that Viv and I were bent on (involving oranges and boys), and presently a voice, 'I think I *could* do a little division, Auntie.' Very soon he was doing quite as well as Viv at it and I praised his success. He then asked leave to go downstairs, and came running up again to his seat to begin another division. 'I wanted to tell Susan that I had done goodly.'

· As a set-off to the morning hour of arithmetic there was a much pleasanter duty for me every evening before the boys went to bed. They demanded a story. For this I had to fall back on any plots I knew, and since they were as anxious as Toddy to have everything as 'bluggy' as possible, it was usually one of the good old tragedies. One night as I was starting *Macbeth* with the usual 'once upon a time' they stopped me to ask how many people were going to get killed. After a hasty mental calculation I said 'Eight'. 'Oooh!' they exclaimed, and settled themselves in joyful expectation.

To keep my brain to the sticking-point their father provided me with a thriller. 'It was written,' said he, 'by a man
called Phillpotts, an old schoolfellow of mine—but it's not
half bad.' I found *The End of a Life* very exciting, and though
I have not seen it since I can even now remember its theme
and many of the details. The villain takes vengeance on his
enemy (a rival in love) by committing suicide in such a way
that it will look like murder for which his enemy will be
hanged. All goes well for the plan and black for the victim.
The novelist's difficulty lay in getting the dastardly plot exposed, and he could do no better than invent a repentant
accomplice. I am sure that a modern detective-story expert
would think up something more subtle.

Until term was over Tom was away at work most of the
day. He never said much about his life at school, and my
knowledge of it comes mainly from old pupils. One of these
writes to me that *awe* was the main feeling they had for him,
and that beside him the headmaster was insignificant. This
was chiefly due to his scholarship and the standard of hard
work that he demanded of the boys, who valued his quiet
approval beyond all praise. The letter goes on to say, '*Every
alteration a mistake* was a grim doctrine rigidly enforced, but
we learnt to live up to it, and it was a most valuable part of
the training we got, to see the end of a sentence before we
put pen to paper.'

The same pupil came to visit the school later on, to observe
various masters at work, as a preparation for his own teaching
career. 'I was not impressed,' he writes, 'by these until I went
to see the Sixth Form Latin. They did one ode of Horace
(iii. 21) and I sat entranced; the University had given me
nothing like it. All that the ode contained was brought out,
the poem was dissected without being mauled and then
reassembled in the other medium with no loss of its appeal.
I never walk through that particular room without hearing
the familiar voice—"O *kindly* jar!" I ought to add that
throughout my schooldays your brother was known as the
one master who had no favourites. He had no moods either,

but was equable and imperturbable, which is very reassuring for schoolboys.'

Another old pupil tells me that Tom never ruled by terror, but rather by surprise and gesture, aided by dry humour, although he never 'made a joke'. He gives as an instance: 'I was once flying downstairs two and three at a time when just at a nasty bend I collided with Mr. Thomas head on. He never said a word, just lifted one eyebrow, gave me a pitying look and passed on his way, while I went on at a reduced speed with my tail between my legs.'

Tom's discipline in class is best summed up in a phrase current among the boys that 'no one *wanted* to fool about in his lessons'. I wonder whether a severe classical training (such as he had at Shrewsbury) does not in itself tend to produce that humorous poise, that ataraxy which nothing else can quite achieve.

Tom's equability was just the same at home as in school. I can recall no instance of annoyance on his part, although little family contretemps were as frequent as with most people. When Christmas Eve came all work was put away, and we laid ourselves out for enjoyment. My own spirits were raised by the post, for I heard that all my students had passed their examination, and that one of them, Miss Pechey, had got a first class in both theory and practice. The boys were excited, for their father took them to the shops to spend their saved-up pocket-money. They had happy recollections of their uncle Barnholt in this matter, for he won their hearts on his last visit to them by decking the mantelpiece every morning with little piles of coppers for them. Dear old Barnholt must have remembered his own childhood, and knew how much more exciting to a small boy are a few coppers that can be spent wildly, than a serious tip to be laid out cautiously under parents' advice or put in a money-box.

While the boys were out shopping Nell and I were left to cope with the food supply. She had accumulated a good store of Christmas cakes, fruits, and sweets, and we had little more to worry about than the goose. After all, this could just go into the oven on Christmas Day. But the butcher had sent with it a huge parcel of giblets, and Nell didn't know what to do with them. Soup was ruled out, because it wouldn't make a complete meal. Then I remembered hearing Arthur talk of his mother's wonderful giblet pies, so I suggested that we should make a giblet pie for the midday Christmas Eve dinner. 'You make the crust,' said I, 'while I wash the giblets and put them in a dish, and Susan makes up the fire.' So we started, but 'What is this stuff?' said I, pointing to some dark purple matter in the parcel. Nell stopped her pastry-making to look. 'Oh, that's blood,' said she, 'I believe you make a kind of forcemeat of it, with crumbs and lemon and parsley.' I protested urgently against this plan, but she said it would fill up the pie and make it go further. As indeed it did.

'Giblet pie!' exclaimed Tom and the boys, when they sat down very hungry after the morning's shopping, 'that's fine!' and they all attacked the generous portions served out.

'What are these balls in the middle?' asked Tom.

'Blood and bread-crumbs, dear,' replied Nell.

Tom shuddered and pushed away his plate. 'I could, if occasion called for it,' said he, 'drink hot blood, but blood and bread-crumbs, no.' Whereupon, of course, the boys with a manly gesture pushed back their plates and refused to touch another mouthful. Nell was furious, and declared that they should have nothing else but bread and cheese. This they contentedly munched while she and I struggled with the pie, which I believe was as distasteful to her as it was to me. Susan did well that day, and I made Nell laugh by telling her of my friend Ursula Wood's remark that economy was one of the two things she most regretted in life. 'What was the other thing she regretted?' asked Nell. 'Tidiness. She said that whenever she tidied her studio she lost hours in looking for things that had been put in their proper places.'

On Christmas morning there was a discussion as to which church we should go to, for Tom was something of a pillar and there were two churches that vied with one another to get him to read the lessons.

'I have to be at St. John's to read the lessons, but you others may prefer St. Cuthbert's.'

'Oh, St. John's please, father,' cried both boys.

Tom noticed that they grinned at one another in a shame-faced way, so he asked for their reason.

'It's because,' said Viv, 'while you are reading the lessons the organist sits on the edge of his rail, and sometimes he gets a bit excited and. . . .'

'Yes, go on,' said Tom, rather pleased at such an effect of his reading.

But Viv stopped and Llew burst in, 'And we always hope he will fall down into the choir.'

Christmas cards and presents kept the little boys happy all the afternoon. I had brought Llew *The Carpenter of Nazareth* (by Bird), fearing that it might be beyond him; but he was an exceptionally thoughtful boy and buried himself in the story, looking up now and again to ask a question. One poser I remember was: 'Auntie, what was there *before* God?' I told him that I didn't know, and that every one wondered and nobody knew. This quite satisfied him.

The next excitement was the pantomime. Tom feared I should be bored with it, but the little boys' delight was pleasure enough. Some of the jokes would certainly not have amused the Queen, and at a specially marked one Tom looked round at me, 'Now, Molly dear, you are getting at first hand the broad humour of the Early Comedy.'

I reminded him of our seeing *Hamlet* together in that theatre years ago, and asked him if the play had ever come to the town again.

'Yes,' said he, 'not long ago; and of course I went to see it. At the first interval a man sitting next me said, 'Do you happen to know if that young fellow in black comes into the play much?' I told him that he came in a good deal and most of the play was about him. 'Well, then, I'm off,' said he, and walked out.

Before I left for London and work again Nelly gave me a piece of sound advice. 'You are too kind to Susan, Molly;

it never does to be too friendly with any one whose life you have to order—because they take advantage.' She was right, of course, but little Susan was hardly one to 'take advantage'. When I laid two half-crowns in her hand as a parting gift, she looked at them in alarm and said, 'You *daren't* give me all that!'

§ 3

My final 'bachelor' holiday was fixed to be spent with Dym in Guernsey. Much had been happening to him since our holidays together in Cornwall. While I was away in America he had become engaged to a Guildford girl. Not long afterwards he obtained a good post in Guernsey, was married out of hand, and took his bride with him to his new home. I had ecstatic letters from him about their small house and strip of garden. It was quite a new experience for Dym to cut and roll the bit of grass, dig the beds, and plant cabbages and peas and beans. He said that every time he came in from College he had to go and see if anything was showing above ground. I had a special letter when the cabbages were visible from the window.

My first visit to them 'to see how they and the beans were going on' had caused me much excitement in the summer of '95. It sounded homely and primitive, this island life among the beans and cabbages. Dym had been too much engrossed in his garden results to tell me anything else, and Bessie's letters had been mainly full of warm welcome and instructions about the voyage. Pooh, thought I, what is such a little voyage after the Atlantic! (but I had not foreseen the Casquets). However, I knew a few things about Guernsey, gathered from school lessons and general chit-chat. It had 'come over with the Conqueror' and belonged to us, but had a government, a language, and a coinage of its own. The people lived by taking in one another's washing. The land was so precious that you weren't allowed to keep poultry because the hens would scratch up the little island. Golf had been forbidden because it involved making holes, intentional and unintentional, in the sacred turf. Old jokes I knew these to be, but my general impression was of a life nearer to nature in the raw than anything I had hitherto met. Nevertheless I decided not to be caught again as I had been in Princetown, and packed not only an everyday and a Sunday dress but also the grand one I had worn at Dym's wedding—just in case.

That first visit to Guernsey had been as great a surprise to me as my first visit to Wales, only the other way about. On going to Wales I expected English conditions, and lo! the simple life. On going to Guernsey I had looked for the simple life, and lo! a civilization more sophisticated than any I had previously known. Society was highly developed, with colonels and majors and naval people in decent plenty. And I think my sister-in-law had made life still more complex by importing some Guildford notions, for Guildford is one of those provincial towns where people know what's what. To begin with the matter of clothes, my three dresses were a mere 'flea in the ocean' when compared with Bessie's wardrobe. For breakfast she had a pretty flowered dressing-gown. At ten she put on a simple business-like tailor-made costume for shopping in Peterport. On returning she changed into a workaday dress and an overall for kitchen operations. The overall was removed for lunch, and then, for the afternoon, a really good dress was put on for paying calls. When we came back a little exhausted from this strain on looking well and being polite, a loose tea-gown was the thing, and this remained on until it was time to dress for dinner. 'Bessie,' I exclaimed in dismay, 'what a lot of changing you go through in one day!' 'Yes, Molly, I do, and it seems a bit troublesome, but I do it from motives of economy. Nothing takes it out of a dress so much as to wear it for a job to which it is not suited.' Truly my two sisters-in-law had widely different notions of economy, and I felt them both to be sound; but I knew that sheer laziness would incline me to follow Nell's example rather than Bessie's.

And the routine for the day was as well planned as the garments. Not a minute was wasted. If I didn't finish my breakfast as soon as Bessie did she brought out her sewing. What I liked best was the morning visit to Peterport; the little up-and-down streets fascinated me, with the glimpses between the houses of the harbour and shipping. I snatched time now and again to do a little sketch while Bessie shopped. Some jolly afternoons were spent in drives round the island; on one occasion this was in an extraordinary vehicle, a kind of combination of bath-chair and hansom cab. I was disappointed to find that there was no wild country, but houses straggling everywhere. I made polite admiration all the time, but enthusiasm, like love, cannot be simulated. 'Molly doesn't seem to be much impressed with our scenery,' said Bessie on our return from one of these excursions. 'Of course she isn't,' replied Dym, 'how can you expect a Cornishman to be stirred by any sea-coast after Hell's Mouth?'

Dym hated anything like sight-seeing, but he was obliged to tog up now and again to pay calls—a role in which I had never seen him before. He suffered gallantly, but refused to 'receive' the return calls. Any knock at the front door would make him rush up to a little room at the top of the house, which he called 'the study' in loving recollection of our old childhood's room in Canonbury—our city of refuge and sanctum. Here he could read and smoke in peace, safe from intruders. But there was one hearty old major who also loved this attic, and if Dym heard his voice he would call to him over the banisters to come up. I liked to listen to the Major's extraordinary stories and used to answer him back and be quite impertinent, to his astonishment and amusement. Meanwhile Bessie was downstairs being polite to his wife. I didn't feel mean, for I was sure that Bessie preferred this to the Major's conversation. I used to busy myself with a bit of knitting while his stories were going on, but I dropped so many stitches and left so many gaps that even the Major raised his eyebrows. I explained it as a new kind of open-work, much in vogue at the moment in London.

This had all been in their early married days. When I went over for my visit in the Easter of '97 I found some changes. For now my little one-year-old godson held the centre of the field. The dressing-gown, the overall, and the négligé

had longer innings. Fewer visits were paid, and the visitors
who came to the house were only those who really wanted
to come. Everything was far more interesting to me than
before, particularly the daily expedition to the town for
shopping. My knowledge of catering was almost limited to
buying eggs and bacon for breakfast, and I was keen to pick
up hints for my forthcoming household needs. The mere
sight of the market was a satisfying artistic pleasure, the flowers,
fruit, and vegetables giving such a profusion of colour. And
how I admired and wondered at Bessie, for she had none of
Nelly's happy-go-lucky style of shopping. She asked searching
questions about the conditions of meat and vegetables, and
gave orders in a clear-headed, decisive way. But one weakness
she confessed to me—the only weakness in her whole character
so far as I saw it. It was fish. Beyond the obvious cod, salmon,
and lobster she didn't know one fish from another. Of course,
in such a port, the fish-stall was always laden with glittering
beauties, and the citizens were supposed to know all about their
species and value. Before that stall Bessie would stand and
point, saying hurriedly, 'Send me up two pounds of that.'

More eagerly than the catering did I watch the management
of the godson, determined to learn all I could. I entered into
the details of food and bath and cot, and heard all the correct
things to do with a baby. In these matters, too, Bessie's organization astounded me. Little Barnholt ate and played and slept
at regular times. For instance, while we were down at the
market it was the servant's duty to take him for his morning
outing. She had a standing order to return from this pram-
parade at 11.55. When I showed surprise at the nicety of this
hour Bessie explained: 'You see, if I say twelve, it sounds as if
somewhere about twelve will do, but 11.55 means punctuality.'
(By the way, I have found this quite a valuable device.) One
day, owing to some little domestic hitch, I was allowed to take
Barnholt for this morning outing. Never before had I been
trusted with a baby entirely to myself, and my nervousness was
increased by Bessie's many injunctions. I was to avoid busy
streets, and hills; the pram must not be jerked at the kerb;

baby's brain must not be over-stimulated by having his attention called to too many things; he must not lean over the side; above all, he must on no account be allowed to go to sleep, for his sleeping hour was from 12 to 1, and if he slept out of doors he would be wakeful at home, just when everybody was busy in the kitchen.

So Bessie set off for the market and I set off with the pram, full of pride, responsibility—and anxiety. It was one of those warm, cloudy, heavy days that people who know Guernsey can readily imagine. I chose quiet streets, as may be supposed, and went fearfully over each kerb. With greater difficulty I abstained from calling attention to some exciting animal episodes, including a kitten up a tree. Now I had hardly navigated two or three streets with complete success when Barney took on that glazed look in the eye that even the inexperienced can interpret. I leant forward and gave him a stealthy push in his middle, at which he perked up a bit. But soon the glazed look returned, requiring another push; another return, another push —a kind of danegeld business. Then, with a pathetic look as much as to say, 'Don't dig me in de ribs, Auntie,' his head slumped forward and he was asleep past recall. I had no heart to poke him any more, but walked him quietly about. As I drew near the house at 11.55 I was wondering what excuse I could put up to pacify Bessie. Suddenly the little trump woke, sat up, smiled, and took notice generally. I said nothing beyond the report that he had been very good and had not got excited by things around him, and I was amused to be told at lunch that he had slept soundly after the outing that Auntie had so carefully taken him.

A little overawed by Bessie's proficiency, I ought to have approached matrimony in a chastened spirit, but I could only keep saying to myself, 'There'll be Arthur about the place, and nothing else matters.'

X
Wedding Without Tears

IN the summer of 1897 the whole country seemed given up
to gaiety. The 'Queen's weather' of glorious sunshine
began to work in the early part of the year and was repeat-
ing the glories of 1887. People from all parts were pouring
into London, all the public buildings and shops were vying
with one another in their decorations, and the coming Jubilee
was the main topic of conversation. The lucky owners of
windows overlooking the route of the procession were making
small fortunes by letting seats.

A seat was quite beyond my means, and I was too old a
Londoner to think of jostling among the crowds in the street.
But luck, as usual, came my way. My ever-constant friends,
M'Jane and Yetta, went to the great expense of hiring two
rooms in Cheapside, high up, with windows giving good
views of the road. This astonished me, for they were always
ostentatious about their radical views, and it seemed incon-
sistent to pay money merely to watch homage being paid to
some one who after all was only a fellow mortal. But at heart
they were as conservative as any one, and almost fanatically
loyal to the Queen, whose joys and griefs they had always
seemed to share. With great forethought they invited some
quite young cousins to see the procession, because these would
be able to remember such an historical event when they were
old. And for no good reason I was asked to share the fun.

And great fun it was. We all started off in two four-wheelers,
M'Jane cumbered with two big baskets. We had to arrive
early, for the streets were closed to traffic some hours before
the ceremony. But there was no dull moment. Cheapside is
historic enough when empty, but the overpowering interest
now was to watch the increasing crowds getting wedged
together and full of good-tempered excitement. Still more

amusing was the way in which every available peep-hole in Cheapside had its spectator: roofs, window-sills, some very perilous-looking ledges, and even chimneys. I guessed that Shakespeare must have seen something of the kind, probably in that very road—always the London route for a triumph.

Meanwhile the true inwardness of M'Jane's baskets was appearing. Cold chicken, tongue, and ham she had thoughtfully placed in sandwiches, so that at any exciting moment we could eat them with still an eye on the window. Lemonade, fruit, and chocolate were always within reach. For later in the day (when the procession should be over and there was a wait before we could get away) she had brought spirit-lamp and kettle for a big sit-down tea.

M'Jane preferred to busy herself in such matters rather than look at the crowds too much, for they made her dazzled and nervous. What an ordeal it must be for any one who is the centre of such a crowd, the one on whom all eyes are strained. The Queen was nearly eighty. Since it was considered easier for her to remain in her carriage than to enter the Abbey, as she had done for the former Jubilee, the open space outside the west door of St. Paul's was chosen as the site for the service of thanksgiving.

We watchers became aware that this service was over and that the procession had left the cathedral, from the indefinable stirring among the crowds below, very much as one becomes aware of the approach of a train from the behaviour of the people on the platform. The rumour, 'They're coming!' seemed to spread from nowhere. We could see the extra craning of necks and could hear the distant cheering, getting ever louder. Presently Captain Ames appeared. He had been chosen to lead the procession because of his great height and fine bearing. After him came long lines of soldiers and sailors of every kind, and from all parts of the Empire. No such representative procession had ever been seen in England before. As each fresh contingent appeared cheers poured forth. At last a roar of almost alarming strength told us that the Queen was at hand. I had not seen her since the early seventies, when she drove along Essex Road (for some obscure reason) and I had been held up to get a view. I then saw a little lady in black and had been rather disappointed that she looked like anybody else. And now the quarter of a century didn't seem to have made much difference to her. It was the same little lady in black, but now she carried a parasol—a merciful protection not only from the blazing June sunshine but also from the sight of so many people perched in perilous spots. Specially engraved on my memory was her personal escort: on one side of her carriage rode her son, our long-beloved Prince of Wales, and on the other side her grandson, the Kaiser—both of them in resplendent uniforms, mostly white. All the brilliance of her surroundings merely emphasized the majesty of the little lady in black.

In all those rejoicing crowds I was the most joyful, for I was to be married early in July. As Arthur and I walked about the streets that evening to enjoy the decorations we regarded them as celebrations of our own crowning mercy. The only one I remember is the device of the old London and North Western Railway, displaying with greatly enlarged capitals, 'Longest, Noblest, Wisest Reign'.

For our wedding we needed no festivities, for the fact itself was feast enough. Nor did getting married present any dire problem. Our chief wealth was the fewness of our wants. The bits of furniture that we each had acquired for our rooms were almost enough to start with, but we were obliged to find somewhere to put them—somewhere to live. We had plenty of advice in this matter from our friends. One section of them said, 'Be sure you have a house, not a flat, because you will want a bit of garden.' The other section urged the advantages of a flat—'Easy to manage, easy to leave for holiday-time, and no stairs.' After looking at endless places of both kinds we fixed on a flat in the middle of Ladbroke Grove, said to be 'six-roomed, with kitchen and bathroom'. When we told the agent who was showing it to us that we could count only five rooms, he pointed to a dark cupboard, suitable for storing trunks, and said, 'This is the servant's room.' I record this to show that such conditions were thought possible for a human being in '97. Arthur was so indignant with the man for suggesting such a thing that he was for walking out at once. I argued that there was plenty of room without the cupboard, and we decided to take the flat, for it was by far the best we had seen. Arthur scrutinized the terms of the lease in order to find some objection, but the only one he could discover was our being forbidden to keep pigeons. 'I don't *want* to keep pigeons,' said he, 'and heaven knows I never shall, but I refuse to be told that I mustn't.' So the clause was deleted.

Nothing then remained to be done but to have our various belongings moved to the flat, from Gray's Inn and the Ladies' Chambers, and supplement them with a few necessities. This involved a short gap for each of us to be homeless. Arthur took some furnished rooms in the neighbourhood of the Temple, and I spent the week with Mary Wood, who had long been promised that I should be married from her home in Camden Road. The idea was that our wedding gathering should consist of Mary and her sister Ursula, and our four brothers—two of Arthur's and two of mine. Since these last were all married, Arthur got one of his bachelor legal friends to act as best man. Custom appears to forbid this office being held by a married man, the reason for which only Frazer knows. Of course, Arthur's parson brother, Llewelyn, was to marry us, Tom was to give me away, and the others were just to rally round and cheer us on. I expect most people have such jolly designs for simplicity, and are thwarted by their friends.

The friend to thwart our little plan was Yetta. She was all for having the whole affair under her management, and for us to be married from her house in proper style. I told her that Mary was my oldest friend, that her house had been like another home to me, and that I had always promised to be married from it. Yetta at once conceded the claims of old friendship. 'Yes, quite right,' said she, 'I wouldn't dream of interfering with such a promise, although M'Jane and I will be greatly disappointed.' I ought to have guessed that this handsome admission was only a retreat to jump the better.

Presently she said, 'You will, of course, *start* from Miss Wood's house, and then I suppose you will be going away somewhere?' I hadn't thought about this, but supposed that would be the idea. 'Surely, then,' said she, 'you could step in for a few minutes after the ceremony to have our good wishes—just on your way to the station? You see M'Jane is not strong enough to go to the Church.' To this I readily assented. Next time I saw her she begged me to send round a few of our presents for M'Jane to see. 'But there aren't any to look at much—mostly tables and chairs and other sensible things that people knew we should want.' 'Well, then, just send a few of the small ones, and make a list of the others, for the people to see.' 'People?' said I, in alarm, my suspicions aroused, 'what people?' 'Only a few. I thought Miss Wood and your brothers might care to come in . . . and one or two other friends, perhaps,' she muttered vaguely. I hung back at this, knowing the brother mind. Then she added, 'Of course, we should have a little light refreshment for them.' At this I protested fiercely, but she flooded me with reasons, and from sheer exhaustion I gave in. When I told Arthur of my capitulation he laughed and said, 'It will please them, and will soon be over. Nothing matters to us. *We* have all the luck.' In a few days I had a letter from Yetta to say that invitations were being sent out, and would I supply a few addresses. The whole thing had become a 'reception'.

'The worst of it is,' I said to Mary, 'that I shall have to dress up to all this.'

'And a good thing, too. And the sooner you set about getting some clothes the better. Let's go off and get the wedding-dress, and lots of other things. You are such a silly about buying clothes, and you mayn't get me to help you like this for ever so long.'

My term at Bedford College ended at the beginning of July, and I had a whole week to spend with Mary having nothing at all to do but enjoy myself. So I fell in with her idea of getting some clothes, and we started off to Derry and Toms'. When it came to discussing the actual wedding-dress I felt obliged to confess that Yetta was designing one of her little cousins to be a bridesmaid. 'In that case,' said Mary firmly, 'you must have something a bit bridal-looking.' 'As long as it isn't white satin and a train and a veil, then.' 'No, only a cream-coloured soft silky thing, walking length, and a picture hat. It will come in quite useful afterwards for a dance or a garden party.' The fact was, I was putty in Mary's hands, and agreed not only to this but to a grey coat and skirt to 'go away' in, as well as a lot of other accessories that Mary thought the right thing for married life. Among these was an extremely bright dressing-gown. The dress-maker was a Frenchwoman, very sympathetic and ready with suggestions. She recommended for the hot weather a little outdoor cape, in this way: "e clothe the shoulder and 'e not make warm.' White gloves, white shoes and stockings—these all seemed to me most extravagant, particularly a white lace handkerchief. When I protested Mary said that I might not be married again for quite a long time.

One of our expeditions during that week was a visit to the church where I was to be married. St. Andrew's, Holborn, we found quite interesting. Its very position was odd, between three streets—Holborn Viaduct, St. Andrew Street, and Shoe Lane. From an old print in the church we saw that it once stood at the top of 'Heavy Hill' (so called because it led from prison to gallows); but since the building of the viaduct one has to step *down* to the entrance. The pulpit had a special interest for us, not because Wesley and Whitefield preached from it (they seem to have done this from every City pulpit) but because of the courage of the rector Hacket during the Civil War. A puritan 'Kensitite' of the time came in one day when Hacket was reading the service and forbade him to go on with it, at the same time pointing a pistol at him and asserting that it was his duty to shoot, because he had been sent by the Earl of Essex. Hacket's reply was simple: 'Very good, you go on with your duty, and I'll go on with mine.' He then resumed his prayers, and of course the soldier retired. Naturally I was interested in the registers, and was glad to learn that a famous lawyer and a famous poet (Coke and Hazlitt) had been married there. We already knew that Disraeli had been baptized there, found out that this had been when he was thirteen, and wondered whether these years had been considered 'ripe' enough for using that special service that we had never heard.

What with one thing and another the days of that week passed happily away, and I forget our other expeditions. Meanwhile Yetta had not been idle. Her organization had been extending. 'As our house is so much nearer the church than Miss Wood's, it would be far better if you and she were to come to lunch here, and then she can dress you here, and change you again here into your travelling-dress. So please have your wedding-dress sent here.' We laughed. 'Yetta's suggestions,' said I, 'are like those of the boarder in *Rudder Grange*—the worst of them is, they are always right.' 'All we shall have to do, then,' said Mary, 'is to spend a leisurely morning here, step into a hansom and go off in time for their lunch. At all events you will still be married *from here*.'

I have had many a jolly drive in a hansom, but that was certainly the jolliest. It was a perfect summer day, and the familiar old streets, that I had often paced along to school with varied feelings, took on that morning an unsubstantial, fairy look.

The lunch was a solemn business, an ordinary midday meal unrelieved by any alcoholic note. Although there were several young cousins around the board, obviously expectant of some fun, I sensed that any levity on my part before the ceremony was misplaced. I was glad when it was over and Mary took me up to a bedroom to 'robe' me, and we could fool about a little in the process. But we felt more solemn when we saw the carriage that Yetta had ordered to take us to the church, and the bow of white ribbon that the driver displayed on his whip. I amused Mary on the way by telling her of Arthur's habit of running everything up to the last moment. 'We shall no doubt see him pelting along Holborn, trying to overtake us.'

As I went down the steps to the church I was overjoyed to see my two brothers, Tom and Dym, grinning a welcome at me. 'Arthur's here all right,' said Dym, 'getting jolly nervous that you won't turn up in time.' Yetta, of course, had gone before me, and as Tom led me up the nave he told me how they had all been amused by her telling him and every one else exactly what they had to do. 'A bit stiff, you know, when it came to informing Llewelyn.' I suppose no woman forgets her last walk in her maiden name, and no woman can have a happier memory of it than I have: on the arm of an ideal brother I was walking to an ideal husband, and as I went was vaguely aware of quite a little congregation of old pupils and students and friends, as well as several of Arthur's barrister friends. Among them I specially noticed, and managed to greet with a smile, Mrs. Keyes, in a brightly coloured new bonnet.

Arthur and his best man, Tom and I, with my little bridesmaid behind, were all present and correct—but no Llewelyn. Yetta grew very restive and was actually making a movement to haul him out of the vestry when he bustled forth and began. There had been a great deal of argument in the press as to whether a woman ought to promise to obey her husband, and some brides had omitted the word. So I said my 'obey' firmly, feeling the pleasure of having no longer to order other people's lives, but to be ordered myself. I still seem to feel the grip with which Arthur 'took' me, and the fierce way in which he pressed the ring home. Llewelyn felt it his duty to give us a short address, but as we had had ten years to consider the matter we hardly needed an exhortation as to our duty; the mere idea of Llewelyn in his canonicals solemnly preaching to us struck me as so absurd that I had to fix my attention on the great east window to keep from laughing.

I had always wondered why people were so long in the vestry after a wedding 'just signing their names'. Now I discovered that there were other little ceremonies apart from the registration business. The atmosphere was completely different from the solemnity by the altar. Even Llewelyn unbent It seems that the best man is entitled to be the first to kiss the bride. But Arthur was too quick for him. Indeed we had fun enough, crowded in that small vestry, but we had no joke to compare with the one at Dym's wedding: his mother-in-law was let loose with the register and signed her name on the dotted line for the 'officiating priest'.

Arthur and I retreated through a back door of the church to one of the lower streets where the carriage was waiting for us. 'A cigarette,' said Arthur, 'I simply must have.' On our return to the house we found M'Jane and a few of her friends assembled in the drawing-room to greet us. 'Miss Thomas and Mr. Hughes,' sang out the parlour-maid as she pompously flung open the door, and then went scarlet at her mistake; but the laughter with which it was greeted was just the pleasantest thing to happen. A crowd of guests were on our heels, and a very jolly reception it was, in spite of its being on a strictly teetotal basis. I was sorry to see that the beautiful carpet had been covered by a drab-coloured drugget, 'in case,' so Yetta explained, 'some one should drop a strawberry.' The few wedding presents available had been spread about to make conversation. Conspicuous among them shone Tony's gift, a pair of Sheffield silver candlesticks that had been made for my Grandfather Vivian untold years ago. Mary Wood's comment on them was: 'With these, Molly, no matter how poor you are, you will always look grand.' My full list of presents was quite imposing. Tom sidled up to me and whispered, 'So sorry, darling, that I've sent you nothing— not even a trifle to put on your list. It was a choice between a present and coming to the wedding, and I didn't think you could be properly married without me.' 'Quite right,' said I, 'but you might just see what I've put on the list.' Arthur's brother Alfred was now very well off, and had given us a big cheque. I recorded it thus: 'A. W. Hughes—cheque'; then next to it I had recorded: 'T. E. Thomas—cheque.' Tom was soon at my side again. 'Molly, you're a brick; I feel like that Ben Adhem chap on the second night, and no one will be so indelicate as to inquire about amounts.'

We had made no plans for going away, leaving our destination to the luck of the moment. Scraps of consultation on the point between Arthur and his best man floated to me now and again: 'But you must have some idea where to go?' 'Well, Tooting sounds absurd, and Ponders End sounds heavy, but beyond these I don't care . . . no, it's no use asking Molly . . . she cares still less.' 'How about Salisbury . . . cathedral and Stonehenge . . . I know a good hotel . . . shall I look up a train and wire for a room? How long are you staying?' 'Only the week-end. I've got a case on Tuesday.' I noticed that a happy look spread over the best man's face at Arthur's willing assent to his making the arrangement, and that he sped off at once on his errand.

I soon faded out of the company for Mary to change me into my travelling garb, and Arthur too had got away some-where to change into a quite old suit and tie much the worse for wear. There were hearty farewells and gratitude to Mary and our kind hostesses, M'Jane and Yetta; our small baggage was put on a cab, and the order 'Waterloo' was given by Dym to the cabby. We thought that we were off by ourselves at last. But that was where we erred. The cabby seemed a bit stupid about the route (not that we cared), and when we reached Waterloo there were the boys to receive us—Tom and Dym, Llewelyn and Alfred, and the best man—as masculine a send-off as any bride ever had. One face among the boys that day was sorely missed by both Arthur and me. His greatest friend, Bourne, our mainstay through our long years of engagement, had recently gone off to South Africa, that whale of a place that swallows our straying prophets and knows better than to cast them home again. He's there still.

It was not the thing in those days for a woman to be served at the buffet, so I was ensconced in the train with some light literature while the six boys went off to have a stirrup cup— medically necessary in Alfred's opinion after the strain of the reception. Later on I was told about that scene in the refresh-ment-room. The presence of parson Llewelyn, and the splen-dour of garments and button-holes, gave rise to knowing glances from every one. Arthur, in his old suit, hung in the background and tried to look like a poor relation. He might well have passed it off thus had he not tried to clinch it by inclining his head towards Alfred and saying to the barmaid, 'That's the bridegroom.' Alfred was the tallest and handsomest of the group, and the best dressed, in grey frock-coat and top hat, carnation in button-hole and, as always, a most captivating smile. But the barmaid was no novice in such scenes and immediately turned the attention of all the room on poor Arthur by saying, 'Oh no, Sir, it's you.'

Whether the proprietress of the County Hotel in Salisbury was as experienced as the barmaid, or whether the best man's telegram had been fuller than necessary (as we suspected), or whether our own faces gave us away, we couldn't tell, but we were received with smiling *empressement*. We appeared to be the only guests, and had the full attention of the staff. After dinner we went to unpack what little luggage we had brought. Mine was all contained in a Japanese basket supported by a strap. I made a little show by spreading out my brilliant dressing-gown and a lovely embroidered night-dress marked 'Mary Vivian', for it had been worked by my mother for her own trousseau. Meanwhile I was aware of Arthur tossing out the contents of his gladstone bag with muttered imprecations. Shaving things, socks, ties, and law papers lay about the room. After a final savage dive into the bag he burst out, 'What d'you think I've done? I've been and forgotten to put in my nightshirt!' An impasse if ever there was. We could do without most things, but the wedding-garment of a nightshirt did seem to come under the head of iron necessities. We rejected almost at once the idea of borrowing one in the hotel, for there was no *maître* in the place. 'Let's go out and buy one,' said I, 'it's still light, and some shop is bound to be open.'

So off we started. Saturday evening in a country town seems to be the same everywhere. Streets congested with idlers. All the respectable shops were shut in the better parts, so we made our way towards the market-place, where the humbler members of the populace were driving bargains over stalls or in nondescript small shops. One of these was larger than the rest, a kind of universal provider, with a very low ceiling from which was festooned every type of garment for the million. While Arthur was short-sightedly peering about I descried a flannelette nightshirt of fierce pink, reduced from two and eleven in black figures to one and eleven in red. When the man pulled it down from its perch we found it even worse to touch than to sight. 'Never mind,' said Arthur, as it was wrapped up, 'it might possibly have been worse; anyhow 'tis enough, 'twill serve.' When we got outside the shop he added, 'Let's get back quick to the hotel with it, lest some accident befall us by the way. We don't want to be found dead with it.' So we did, only to find later that it had been opened out by the chamber-maid and ostentatiously placed beside my dream of old embroidery.

Down we went into the town again, where last shoppings had now given way to sheer loafing and merriment, just suiting our mood. An old fellow with a kind of fiddle was actually playing 'Land of my Fathers', was able to reply when Arthur hailed him in Welsh, and was delighted with the largesse he received. This reminded Arthur of an incident that he had enjoyed a year or two before. He was walking in a street of Cardiff with a reverend old professor of the university, when they came across a man playing the fiddle vilely. Arthur asked him to lend the fiddle a minute, and taking it struck up a lively Welsh jig. Clients rolled up from surrounding streets, and the man's hat overflowed with coppers. Arthur was quite pleased at the result of his performance, but on looking round he discovered that he was not the main attraction. The old professor had picked up his coat-tails and was dancing in the roadway. He said he hadn't enjoyed himself so much since he was a boy.

It had been a cloudlessly sunny day, and now the moon had risen; it was nearly, but not quite, at its full. Nature does sometimes appear to reflect and enhance our own emotions. The cathedral drew us like a magnet. Surely there are few spots on earth to surpass in beauty that grassy Close, surrounded by dignified old houses, and in the midst the most graceful of spires to dominate the country round. We were almost frightened by our complete happiness. 'The worst of it is,' said Arthur, 'that one of us is sure to go before the other.' Then I told him how mother had asked me once: 'Which would you rather, that Arthur should die first or yourself?' and when I said at once 'Myself,' she replied, 'Well, then, you don't love him enough yet.'

XI

Ordinary Struggles

§ I

MOST newly married women have the same difficulties to meet: servants or the lack of them; finding good provision shops; keeping expenditure down; making the daily routine run smoothly in the new surroundings. I had my share of all these, and made a fair crop of mistakes.

We returned from Salisbury on the Monday afternoon, and spent the rest of the day in pottering about the flat, putting up pictures, sitting on packing-cases, and revelling in the bare fact of having a home of our own. For supper we went out to a little restaurant. Miss Rogers's present had been a large lamp, and fortunately I had laid in a supply of oil; it was therefore possible for Arthur to sit up and have a last go at his brief for the next day. So it was not till the following morning that my troubles began.

There was no gas in the flat (nor ever was for the seven years we lived in it). Now I had been accustomed to do marvels on the little gas-ring in the Ladies' Chambers—cook porridge, fry bacon, scramble eggs, and even make a stew. And here I was faced with a huge iron range for my first attempt at a breakfast. Disraeli said that there were three things a man should never grumble at because they were unalterable—the weather, his wife, and the kitchen range. But I think he would have let loose a few expressions if he had been in my shoes. I had got up early, lit the fire, filled the kettle, arrayed slices of bacon in the pan, only to be met by smoke billowing forth at me from my 'fire'. In despair I called out to Arthur for help. He just shoved a damper or two about, and that impish range, seeing a man on the job, gave up its tricks and blazed up brightly. I felt that it was like the nursery rhyme 'stick won't beat dog':

everything began to hum—kettle began to sing, bacon began to frizzle, cloth was laid, and, best of all, Arthur had been got out of bed in good time.

As soon as he had started for the Temple I was busy enough. Most of my time was spent in unpacking cases, pushing things into place, and tidying away the oceans of packing-paper and straw that surged around. I couldn't make a bonfire, and I didn't dare to irritate my range. I thought of the story, that puzzled me as a child, of the old woman whose square house became round; the explanation being that she thrust everything into the corners. Then there was the servant's room to get ready, for she was to come on the following day. I had a rooted idea that a servant's bedroom must have pink chintz covered with muslin round her table. With some trouble I had managed to buy these things beforehand; and now I had but to nail them on to a little table, make up her trestle bed, and lay out her caps and aprons.

A friend had recommended to me a girl of eighteen, from East Dereham, in Norfolk, and I had made arrangements to meet her at the terminus on the following afternoon. I found Emma a fresh-faced, cheerful country girl. She had never before left her village, and told me that she had liked the journey, but had been dreadfully afraid, as the train rushed through several stations, that it wouldn't stop at London. The streets made no impression on her as we drove out to Ladbroke Grove, but she was astonished at the seventy steps that led up to our front door, and quite alarmed at her first venture forth alone: 'I didn't know where that road was going to, mum.' On her second venture she came rushing up the stairs again in great distress: 'I met a funeral, mum. Oh, I couldn't have went. Down hoom it means a death in the family.' As there was a cemetery at the end of the road, I had to kill this superstition at once.

Emma's turns of speech fascinated me, especially the Norfolk idioms. One neat phrase was an absolute 'do', equivalent to the clumsy 'if it should happen'. Thus she would say, 'I hope it won't rain, do we can't go'. She used the word 'deen' for any small quantity, but always in the negative: 'There's not a deen of sugar left'—'We've not heard a deen of the postman.' She sang, more or less all day long, odd snatches of hymns and popular songs. I was besought at all hours to count my blessings, name them one by one, and told that I should be surprised at what the Lord had done—a bit irritating when the milk had just boiled over. An organ-grinder was one day playing a tune that I failed to recognize, and I asked her what it was. She at once diagnosed it as 'Say Olive Oil'. 'How queer,' said I. 'Why say olive oil? How does it go on?' 'Say olive oil, say not good-bye.' And then, of course, I gathered its meaning from the context. Sometimes of an evening, when Arthur was at work, the singing was trying. 'I shall have to stop it,' said I; but Arthur wouldn't allow that. 'Let her sing while she can,' said he, 'the time may come when she has no heart for it.'

Emma was a treasure. She not only knew how to work, but knew what to work at—a still more valuable asset. For I was ignorant in this line. I had vague ideas that servants were busy all the time, but what they were busy at was a mystery. Emma had a special day for 'turning out' each room, always cleaned the silver on Friday, and devoted Saturday to the kitchen. As for washing, I wished she had kept a special day for that, but she had a penchant for washing, and would wash at all hours. Things that seemed to be spotless would go into the tub if I turned my back. When I protested that the poor towels and pillow-cases were getting done to death by this ruthless washing, she laughed and said 'That's just what father says, because down hoom mother is always scrubbing. "If the landlord only knew it," he says, "he'd put five pounds on to the rent for what you take out of the house by for everlasting cleaning it."' I could see that Emma liked me to go out, so that she could get on with her work faster, and surprise me with her results on my return.

I had to leave her alone nearly every morning while I went out to do the shopping. Bessie of Guernsey, of mature experience, had advised me to get everything at Whiteley's.

'You've only got to walk into the shop, order what you want in the different departments, and you find everything delivered at your door.' She was right, but I soon found that this easy way of buying had to be paid for by too high prices, so I determined to explore the neighbourhood, buy what I wanted, and bring it home myself. There were actually some shops on the ground floor of our flat, but not of the right kind. One was a tailor's. But I never saw any symptom of tailoring going on, nor any customer going in. The shop row was one of those in London that seem doomed to failure for no assignable reason. One day Arthur found to his amusement, scrawled in chalk on the pavement, the words 'Lord have mercy upon us'. This was not intentional sarcasm about the shops, but was probably the work of a pious old fellow who used to stride to and fro in Notting Hill and say urgently into one's ear as he passed, 'Do you love Jesus?' I used to answer 'Yes, indeed' to cheer him, for I fear he suffered much from small boys.

One fortunate morning I found, quite a short distance away, another of London's oddities. It was a complete contrast to our row of respectable shops—no outward attractions and yet enjoying the liveliest trade. In an old narrow winding lane, once no doubt a medieval thoroughfare, I found shops and stalls catering for those who have no money to waste and mean to get the utmost value for their outlay. They were not to be put off with stale vegetables or doubtful fish—such as I had experienced in the 'better-class' shops. I expect Bessie would have been shocked to see me coming home with my booty, for, of course, nothing was 'sent up'.

One shop, a greengrocer's, was the most satisfactory place of business I have ever been in, for there seemed to be no waste at all. It had been so successful that it had spread out into an enormous rambling store, and was always crowded with customers. The premises were allowed to remain ramshackle, no books were kept, no credit given, and the whole energy of the staff was devoted to getting the best they could every morning from Covent Garden and selling it quickly at a small profit. By the 'best' I don't mean exotic fruits or anything out of season, but great piles of all that was 'in'—such as fresh strawberries, raspberries, currants—served out to the first comers (often little children) with good humour, homely manners, and very little wrapping up. Once I had already filled my shopping basket when I spied some sprouts and begged for a paper bag to put them in. 'Not for greens, my dear,' was the inexorable reply.

Meat I preferred to buy in another road, for the joints and pieces in the lane were turned over by prospective buyers. But fish was always safe. 'Are those soft roes?' I asked a huge woman who was presiding over a mountain of fresh herrings. 'I won't deceive you, my dear,' said she, 'they ain't.' How she managed to have such an intimate knowledge of every one of them was a puzzle to me, till Arthur explained that the soft roes are sorted out at Billingsgate, as being more valuable. He took great interest in the scraps of experience that I related to him in the evenings. They added to his apparently inexhaustible store of odd information—mostly derived first-hand from contact with the people he met, from judges to tramps. On a railway journey once with a commercial traveller, he entered into the difficulties, disappointments and even tricks of the trade, to such an extent that the man couldn't believe that he hadn't done some 'travelling' himself. This propensity to talk to every one came from sheer interest in life, with no ulterior motive, but, of course, his uncanny acquaintance with a man's daily routine was of great use when a witness was cross-examined, for the unexpected knowledge would surprise a liar into truth.

One incident of my shopping specially amused us both. After buying some candles one day in a tiny 'Italian warehouse' in the lane, I noticed that the woman was doing up the parcel very slowly, and stopping to look up at me woefully. 'Anything the matter?' I asked. 'Oh, do tell me,' said she, 'what to have for dinner; my husband's a bit hard to please.' 'How about a steak?' 'Has that nearly every day; wants a bit o' change.' 'A haddock?' 'Had that yesterday.' I launched out,

'Why not give him a mixed grill?' 'What's that?' 'You can change it about as you can get the things; but you have a nice slice of fried bread, and arrange on it and round it a couple of sausages or kidneys or a cutlet, and then add bacon and a bit of liver, tomatoes, mushrooms. . . .' As I grew lyrical her face brightened and her thanks were so profuse that I felt like the man who helped Simon Lee.

Shopping in the lane brought my accounts down nicely, and I kept them rigidly, noting every item, such as 'parsley —$\frac{1}{2}d$.' Everything was paid for by me except coal and Emma's wages, and I received thirty shillings from Arthur each Monday morning, frequently having four or five shillings in hand against the unforeseens of the following week. Clothes were little worry to either of us, for thanks to Mary Wood I had stocked myself well, and Arthur's method of replenishing his wardrobe was simplicity itself. Ever since his Cambridge days Mr. Neal, of Trumpington Street, had supplied him with clothes, and as far as I could judge Arthur paid him for this marvellous service £5 a year, at the same time always owing him about £20. As I had a horror of the smallest debt I suggested that Arthur should pay off the whole. 'Pay it all!' he exclaimed, 'What a blow it would be to Neal! He would think that I was dissatisfied and finished with him.' So I hoped it would never be paid, for apparently nothing but the death of a customer would excuse such an act of discourtesy. A man's method of choosing new clothes seemed to me equally strange, and its simplicity charmed me. Mr. Neal paid periodical visits to his customers in London, told them what they wanted, and took orders; in due course the parcel arrived at home. 'Saw old Neal in the Temple to-day,' Arthur would tell me, 'and he says I want a new overcoat as well as a new suit. I suppose I do. He showed me a lot of patterns for the trousers—they seem to be the only things one can have any choice about. But these were so much alike that I asked him why he didn't break out into something fresh. "The taste of the public," said he solemnly, "appears, Sir, to have settled in stripes."' This kindly man was more of a friend than a tailor to both of us, taking genuine interest in the joys and sorrows of our life; and now his sons clothe my son Arthur in the same delightful way.

§ 2

Cooking was the main field of my ambition, and it took me hours of thought and many failures before I managed to do it with half my mind, as one ought to do. Cookery books were little use for a beginner, never saying how to do the common things, such as making gravy out of nothing. Two guiding stars were the outcome of my own experience: (1) Never to keep Arthur waiting for his meal. (2) Never to give him cold mutton.

Gazing dubiously one day at a saucepan of stew, I heard Emma's voice behind me, 'The Consul's brow was sad and the Consul's speech was low.' 'Good gracious!' said I, 'where did you pick up that?' 'Oh, we learnt that at school.' She was eager to learn anything she could, and one day when I had to go some distance to pay a call she begged me to let her manage the whole dinner—joint and vegetables, pudding and all. I risked it, and at her urgent request didn't return till just upon dinner-time. It was a complete success, and I shall never forget her look of pleasure when Arthur proclaimed it 'top-hole'.

Many a bit of country lore I picked up from Emma. One of these described the ideal wife:

> *She could make, she could bake,*
> *She could brew, she could sew,*
> *And found time to teach her three sons to say 'No'.*

Brewing was out of my scope, and so were the three sons at the moment, but what about baking? I determined to have a try at this. My cookery book was discouraging, making it seem that to cook a loaf of bread was like carrying out some chemical experiment, referring to weights (I possessed no scales) and even to Fahrenheit. So I harked back to my recollections of having seen it done scores of times in Cornwall and Wales, without having paid attention to the actual details. I remembered how often mother used to send me out when I was a little child to buy a pennyworth of yeast at the baker's, for her saffron cake. So I sent Emma out on a like errand. She had never made bread, but recalled a saying of her mother's —'All that bread wants is time and warmth.' I started in with some flour; the yeast and the oven did their work; and with beginner's luck I produced some lovely rolls. These were placed on the table within reach of Arthur at dinner.

'Good roll, this,' said he, trying one. 'Where do you get them? A new baker?'

'Yes,' said I, as casually as my bursting pride would allow me, 'I made them myself.'

'Do you mean to tell me,' he exclaimed, 'that this thing is only flour and water?' Holding it up in amazement, he added, 'Then what on earth do they do to the bread in the shops?'

To this day I have never gone back from that exciting discovery, and except in emergencies have produced my own bread for over thirty years, the family strongly objecting to 'boughten' bread. People dislike the idea of trying this for themselves because of the 'time it takes'. The bread certainly wants time, I assure them, but not *their* time; it doesn't ask to be watched, and can be trusted alone in the house; the actual labour in making a batch takes about six minutes from start to finish. But they shake their heads in a melancholy way as they ask for another slice.

An old friend of Arthur's, Dr. Daniell, learned in physics and indeed everything else, was quite excited about the bread, wanted to hear exactly how I made it, but was shocked at my having to send out for the yeast. 'Why not save time and trouble, not to mention expense, by making your own?' he urged. So, following his directions, I cooked two pounds of potatoes, mashed them up in water and all, poured them into an earthenware pan, and when they were cooled to about blood heat, placed a slice of toast to float on the top with an ounce of yeast spread on it. (After all, one had to *begin* with a bit of yeast.) After some hours the whole panful became yeast, and we bottled it and put it away, using from it as required. Economical, labour-saving, efficient. But Arthur said it must stop, because his nerves couldn't stand it. It was frequently his custom of an evening to be sitting up late for work after I had gone to bed, Emma had ceased singing, and all was quiet. Once, at about midnight, he was startled by what he called an infernal explosion. One of the bottles of yeast had burst its cork forth. So we returned to the pennyworth of yeast at the baker's. Another pestiferous visitor, a 'notable housewife', informed me in a superior way that no bread was really home-made unless brewers' barm was used. So I bought a little covered tin can (such as navvies use for their tea) and made expeditions to a brewery for a pennyworth of barm. We could perceive no difference in the quality of the bread, and I found the barm so temperamental and uncertain in its raising power that I soon returned to the original yeast, of which a pennyworth lasted for three bakings.

I wrote continually to my beloved aunt Tony in Cornwall, telling her of my ups and downs, and getting hints from her. She sent directions for stewing a rabbit, and for making a pork-pie, but she considered that I should never be able to achieve the latter. This put me on my mettle, and I made some fine ones; and when she sent me some of her own butter I was able to display an all home-made breakfast.

§ 3

In addition to the fun of shopping and attempts at new cookery, I had people to see me. Not the perfunctory kind, for it was pleasant to reflect that they would never mount those seventy steps in the hope of finding no one at home. There was always plenty to talk about, for if conversation flagged we had one exhibit of constant interest. Our windows looked right down into the grounds of a convent. I forget the name of the sisterhood, but it was a very close one. The nuns never left the premises, ate no meat, and grew all their own vegetables. We had this information from our doctor, who also attended them; he told us that some one had mistakenly sent them a turkey one Christmas, and that they had given it to him. We used to watch them digging and hoeing and watering, and often leaping about over the beds from sheer *joie de vivre*. Then there were frequent processions with chanting, and on special days coloured banners, figures, and crosses were carried round the paths.

One of my earliest visitors must have thought me very queer, for my mind was quite off the subject in hand. I could by no effort remember what her wedding present to me had been; and I felt sure she was expecting some grateful reference to it. It wouldn't do to say merely, 'How good of you to send me that nice present—so useful!' when she was probably sitting on it, eating off it, or gazing at it. No sooner had I seen her off and returned into the room than the little clock on the mantelpiece winked at me and said 'It's me'. For years I've puzzled over the fact that trying to remember a thing puts a stopper on one's brain, and can only conclude that the fussy struggle throws a sabot into the machinery. Perhaps at this time my exuberant happiness affected my memory, for the first time I repaid one of these early calls I couldn't think what my name was when the servant asked me.

The wife of a doctor (not our own) during the course of her visit told me how she suffered from young women patients who adored her husband and were always haunting the surgery with some feigned complaint. 'Thank goodness,' I replied, 'there's no trouble of that kind with a barrister.' 'Ah, Mrs. Hughes,' said she, shaking her head sadly, 'you *little* know what goes on in the Temple!'

Far more pleasant than such callers as this was the dropping in of kindred spirits—our brothers and their wives, our Celtic cousins, old friends on their visits to London, and the ever-welcome Mary Wood and her sisters. M'Jane and Yetta even mounted those stairs to give me encouragement and advice, to bring me some extra comforts or labour-saving gadgets, rearrange the furniture, and instruct Emma how to be more

correct in her way of bringing in the tea. Sometimes I found
these alterations and suggestions a bit trying, but Arthur said,
'Never refuse advice. Whether you follow it or not is another
matter.'

Most of my old companions were content to be amazed
and amused that my *ménage* worked at all, and we exchanged
notes on our experiences. My Cornish cousin Lucy, whose
varied homes had included both Norway and China, compared
my conditions very favourably with her own newly married
life.

'We started from Cornwall with some nice new furniture,
but our route lay through the Straits Settlements, and when
we arrived up-country and examined our belongings we found
that the glue had melted, and packing-cases, chairs, tables,
chests of drawers—everything was reduced to a mass of confused sticks.'

Her sister, Christina, also came to see me. She, too, had
travelled in strange regions. Her stories tended to be more
picturesque than Lucy's, but I like to think that this one was
true. She wanted to show her Chinese servant how to answer
the door and announce a visitor properly. After instructing
him verbally, she went outside to rehearse the whole affair
by pretending to be a visitor. She knocked, Wong opened
the door, showed her in and announced her perfectly. It was
her afternoon 'at home', and she then sat down to await any
callers, feeling satisfied that Wong would do his duty properly.
Presently there was a knock, but it was followed by no movement on Wong's part. The knock was repeated. Still dead
silence within. A third knock roused her to anger and she
went to the door herself to find Wong outside, grinning. 'You
foolie me,' said he, 'me foolie you.'

Another cousin was the mother of several boys, and told
me that once during a visitor's call there came through the
open window an agonized cry as of a child being torn by
machinery. Rushing out she found her son laughing with
delight at the success of the noise that some Cornish imp had
taught him. She said she wished she were able to achieve the

nonchalance of a certain mother who exclaimed when she heard a blood-curdling yell, 'Thank heaven, one of my sons is still alive!'

My late students of Bedford College who managed to come over to see me were pleased, I'm sure, to be able to turn the tables on me by giving me instruction in domestic work. They knew much more about sewing than I did, and taught me how to cut out, how to place a pocket, put in sleeves, and other mysteries. As for knitting, I could soon turn a heel, and was able to make quite elaborate patterns in fleecy white wool. Arthur assured me that he could knit too, but didn't hold with patterns. One evening when I was making a little woolly jacket of basket-pattern I left it to go into the kitchen. On my taking it up again I found that Arthur had done a row to help me. 'But it's all wrong for the pattern,' I cried. 'No matter,' said he, 'you'll find such quaint aberrations all the thing in really artistic work. Look at the Persian rug. And the small wearer won't notice the oddity, you'll see.' So I kept it. Arthur had no knowledge of domestic affairs, much to my contentment, but if anything went wrong he was on the spot at once with precise efficiency. (How do men do it?) He used to assert that he could make an omelet, had indeed done so once in his bachelor rooms. But I didn't test him, and no crisis ever befell us in which an omelet was called for.

At rare intervals we invited a choice friend or two to come and have dinner with us. Our guests would enter into the spirit of the thing and we all enjoyed ourselves—Emma not least, for she came out strong with her waiting. But once the friends were a little too choice. Dr. Daniell was a man of unlimited anecdote, and an accomplished raconteur. So we selected two other men we knew who were also gifted (or cursed) in this way, hoping that the conversation would be tip-top. Each indeed arrived all primed with his best stories, but, as we ought to have foreseen, he only listened to the others in order to chip in with his own. As for Dr. Daniell, he appeared to know every single story, and couldn't disguise his knowledge of it. After one contribution he said,

'Ah, yes, that is the Norfolk variant.' But nothing deterred them from unloading all their goods, and it was a late hour when they finally tore themselves away. Then, indeed, Arthur and I had the first honest laugh of the evening, as we vowed that we didn't want to hear another funny story ever.

Occasionally Arthur would announce, 'Shan't be home to dinner to-morrow; Alfred's in town.' At other times the reason would be, 'Llewelyn is coming up to see how the bishops are behaving themselves at some blooming meeting.' Or, 'It's call night at the Inn.' Or, 'It's Grand night.' Or, 'The Bacon Club are having their annual dinner.' I used to get much vicarious pleasure from hearing what they had had for dinner, especially after a Grand night at the Inn. I also got much amusement from Arthur's report—always disparaging.

'Not much of a dinner, just mutton, you know.'

'Saddle?'

'Yes, it was saddle, but the jelly wasn't up to much.'

'Asparagus?'

'M-yes, but not enough of it.'

'Ices?'

'M-yes, but I've tasted better, and anyhow I much prefer the dinner I get at home.'

His friends used to tease him about his frequent excuse for declining an invitation—'Sorry, but I've got to get home.' He told me that one of them had accused him of being hen-pecked. 'I always go one better when people get funny, so I told him that it was not much use being married unless one was henpecked a bit.'

On one most memorable day I went to a banquet with him. It was some very specially red-letter day in the life of the Society of Cymmrodorion, of which Arthur was a zealous member. Eminent Welshmen from all parts and in all walks of life were gathered in the big hall of the Holborn Restaurant, to rejoice together in belonging to a nation that had produced so many heroes and poets. Of the long dinner I remember only the oysters—things I had heard of long enough, but never met before. Of the lovely Welsh singing that accompanied the feast I welcomed my favourite 'Suo gân'. The speeches were a delightful mixture of learning and wit. Of course the toast-master was a new experience for me, and his solemnity and pomposity amazed me. The chief guests of the evening for whom he prayed silence were Balfour and Lloyd George. We guessed that these two had never before sat down to a meal together, and the mere fact of seeing them in such close amicability was entertainment enough—as though one should see a lion and a lamb sharing a drink out of a trough. There was no doubt as to which was the lion and which the lamb. Balfour was there because he was steeped in Welsh literature, and Lloyd George was there because he was Welsh (although Arthur pretended to doubt even this!) It was the time when these two were going for one another hammer and tongs almost daily in Parliament. At the dinner their speeches were decorated by gracious bowings to one another and smiling allusions to Another Place. Cleverly as Lloyd George could score off Balfour in debate, he was no match for him in expatiating on the beauties of Welsh poetry, in quoting it, comparing with Homer, and suchlike subtleties, and as soon as decency permitted he left the table on account of 'pressing duties in the House'.

For me the best bit of the evening was the period before the dinner, an ever memorable *quart d'heure*, when all the good and great were mingling and chatting. I could hardly believe that I was within touch of Balfour. Among the cheery throng was one of the most famous judges of the day, a Welshman, and Arthur brought me along for a few words with him. I was too nervous to take in the nice things he was saying to me, but noticed that they included a compliment on Arthur's advocacy. However, I managed to say, 'I have seen you on the Bench.' 'Then I do trust,' said he, in anxious tones, 'that I was behaving myself properly.'

§ 4

The evening was the part of the day that made the rest of it worth while. After dinner we began it with a game of chess, no matter how pressing any work might be. Arthur said it was good for his brain to think of something different, though if he lost he would say, 'My mind was in the Temple.' Now and again, in small ways, I was able to help with his work, usually by dictating passages from a fat law book for some bit of conveyancing. I soon came to be able to read the strange abbreviations which at first made the pages look like a foreign language.

'Conveyancing seems a dull job,' I remarked, after one of these spells of dictation.

'Yes,' said Arthur, 'you just have to peg away at it. It's like your hemming round the bottom of a skirt—you have to be careful, however monotonous it is, for if you slip just one stitch you may get tripped up.'

'A lot of it seems mere verbiage to me,' said I.

'That's what most people think, and that's why we toast the man who makes his own will. He thinks he can put his intentions so simply that he doesn't need a lawyer, and we get a harvest of litigation to clear up his mess. No, believe me, every word in a legal document is necessary. If you leave out some absurdly remote contingency in a will, that contingency will go and happen.'

Arthur's casual manner with a paper marked URGENT surprised me. 'Oh, there's no hurry about that; they usually mark things urgent; it doesn't mean anything.' 'What do they put, then,' I asked, 'if it really is urgent?' as I raked my mind for a stronger word. 'Tuesday morning, 10.15,' said Arthur. 'Quite simple.'

'What do you do,' I asked, 'when they're in a hurry for an opinion, and you want more time to make up your mind?'

'I ask for more information on some point, and while they are getting it I can look up other cases, and so on.'

What I enjoyed most was the discussion of some impending case. The point of view of Arthur's client always seemed to me unassailable, until he trained me to throw all my weight into the enemy's camp. 'It's not a bit of use to agree with me,' he would say. 'I know *my* good points. What I want you to

see is the horribly good point of the other chap, or some
horribly weak one of mine.' He told me how many a case was
ruined by the failure of a client to confess some silly thing he
(or usually she) had done. This, of course, would come out
in cross-examination, and no defence would be ready. People
seemed to imagine that anything written in haste would be
destroyed in haste. 'Remember this, Molly, never write a
letter to any one when you are angry, or if you have any difference with them at all. If write you must, always have legal
advice.'

There was hardly a case that didn't widen our knowledge of
things in general. For instance, there was one about brandy,
in the course of which even Arthur's hair was raised at the
revelations as to its manufacture. Certain 'brandy' was sold
without any ingredient that one would expect. Arthur surmised
that if grapes had ever entered it at all, they must have gone
through on stilts. Our conclusion was that the emergency
brandy we always kept in the cupboard must be the best.

One case was almost amusing from the mere fact of its being
completely hopeless. 'Why didn't you settle it out of court?'
said I. 'Of course I tried to, but the other side know they are in
the right and they are out for blood.' 'Well, what can you do
then?' 'Oh I'll give the defendant a run for his money. I'll
tousle them up and down a bit.' It was in some County Court
at a little distance, and I was surprised to see Arthur back
earlier than usual, and brimming with quiet joy. He related
with glee how he had actually 'pulled off' the case. Everything
was in trim, many witnesses for the plaintiff had been drawn
from far, the stage was all set, and no possible loophole for the
defendant, when Arthur popped up and submitted quite quietly
that, owing to the precise locality of the accident, the court
was the wrong one for the case and had no jurisdiction in
the matter. The whole thing collapsed at once, and the
game was not worth the candle for its renewal elsewhere.
'And serve the man right,' said Arthur, 'for not being willing
to settle.'

This matter of settling out of court meant a severe mental

and moral struggle sometimes. Arthur was for the plaintiff once in a case against a very well-known public man, who had treated an attractive girl in a shabby and dishonourable way. Although it was ostensibly a question of payment for service rendered, the man had written such a lot of ludicrous letters that Arthur knew that he could make London laugh by quoting from them, and that it would easily be a *cause célèbre*, and the making of him. We both got excited over it. But one evening Arthur returned in a dejected state. 'I'm afraid we shall have to settle,' said he. 'I can't entirely trust my client to have told me all that she herself said or wrote, and they are offering a tremendous sum to settle.' 'Yes, but', I protested, 'if they are offering such a lot it means they are in a big funk. Can't you risk it? It would mean such a chance for you.' Arthur's anger with me for suggesting that he should put his own interest before his client's was for me a means of measuring the temptation he had overcome.

Criminal work he determined not to touch, and this decision was final after his one experience of it. A fellow barrister was in a hole with clashing cases, and asked him to take on the defence of a girl charged with child murder. How he slaved one night over a book on medical law! He had been to see the poor girl in prison, and the whole thing had been too much for his feelings, and there were actual tears of indignation in his eyes as he told me about it. By throwing doubt on the evidence of the prosecution as to the state of the child's lungs, and showing that there was a possibility that there had never been full life at all, he managed to get the woman discharged. 'No doubt,' he said to me when he came home, 'they were glad enough to be given any excuse to clear her. But it's no wonder that the men who take up criminal work take to drink. I hear that they all do. No more of it for me.'

Work was always uncertain; frequently two cases would be on at once, and then perhaps a fortnight would go by with nothing on at all. I was told in later years, when things were rather more steady, that early disappointments had been many and bitter; but these had been hidden from me, while good

news was told at once. In fact my only grievance against
Arthur was that he protected me from the unpleasant rather
too much. I came from an enduring stock, and would have
preferred to share the rubs as well as the boons. One rub,
however, he felt obliged to disclose. We had been having a
specially pleasant little dinner party at home, with Mary Wood's
eldest sister and her husband. They were both artists and
travellers and provided delightful conversation till late in the
evening. When they had gone Arthur said, 'I've got something rather dreadful to tell you . . . I had my pass-book in
to-day from the bank, and what do you think we are reduced
to?' 'Tuppence ha'penny?' said I. 'Well, not much more,
only just over £7.' 'It might be worse,' said I, 'anyhow we
aren't in debt for anything, and some fat work is bound to come
in soon.' And so it did, for not long after this he came home
with the news that a brief had come in marked 100 guineas.

I suppose it is the same in every calling, that a man suffers
almost as much from its petty annoyances as from the uncertainty
of the income it brings him. Arthur's Leaders not only
tortured him by sometimes spoiling a good point, but would
often expect the Junior to do all the preliminary work without
contributing much themselves. 'Look at this so-called opinion
he has sent in,' said Arthur, in exasperation, one day. 'I should
think he did it while he was shaving.'

In his early days at the Bar Arthur had suffered much from
unprincipled solicitors, who got advice and hours of work
without intending ever to pay for it, knowing that a barrister
has no redress for this kind of theft. Although he had many
staunch friends among solicitors, such knavish treatment
soured him towards them as a class, and yet he was obliged
to 'nurse' them. He told me an absurd story of a barrister
friend of his who invited a solicitor to lunch and plied him
with food and wine, and was not a little surprised to find his
guest anxious to pay for the whole thing. It was not until the
coffee and cigar stage that they discovered that both of
them were barristers under the delusion that the other was
a solicitor.

The patronizing manner of some of the solicitors was their most annoying feature, and the fiery-tempered Arthur needed all his self-restraint to keep decently polite. One night I was awakened by a violent kick. 'Hold!' cried I, 'what now?' 'Sorry, darling,' came a sleepy voice, 'I thought you were a solicitor.'

XII

Bronwen

WHEN life hums happily along one day seems much the same as another, in retrospect. But an unusual event revivifies the preceding incidents, and the trivialities just before the greatest day of my life stand out as though they had happened yesterday.

One morning in the late spring of '98 I went out to do my usual shopping in Portobello Lane, and captured a fine piece of cod for the evening meal, and some shrimps to make a sauce for it. Then I bought oranges at the famous greengrocer's, where I had on one occasion bought eight good oranges for a penny. The pudding was to be Arthur's favourite, a marmalade one, called Sir William Watkins. This was always a bit of a gamble, but to my relief it turned out finely, and as it was backed up by cheese straws and coffee, all went well. Then we settled down to our usual game of chess. Annoyed at being beaten, though it was my usual fate, I demanded another game and a chance for revenge. No good. So then Arthur settled to his law work and I to my 'parlour work'. We gave this name to any kind of sewing, from a story of my mother's. She had invited an old servant to come to tea, and the reply was :'Thank you, mum, I'll come when I have a bit of parlour work that I can bring.' When she came she brought a pair of her husband's trousers to mend.

I felt a bit tired and went to bed early, and about half an hour later I tapped on the wall to summon Arthur for a consultation, as I called it. He thought he had better have a second opinion, and ask the doctor to look in. Since the latter lived quite close he was soon on the spot, and dispatched Arthur to fetch the nurse (who, of course, like all nurses, was at another case in some remote suburb). Before starting Arthur called up Emma and told her to light the fire in the special room prepared for the emergency, to get me into it, and to sit with me until he returned with the nurse. Emma was as excited as myself, delighted to speculate with me on all the possibilities ahead, as we chatted away the time in the firelight. Most reluctantly she returned to bed when the nurse arrived, at two o'clock.

Even at that forbidding hour the energetic little nurse felt that she ought to be doing something or asking where something was. I understood the expression 'snatches of sleep', for all I got that night was really snatched from a running fire of questions, washings, combings, and straightenings. A spread of small bustling surrounded the nurse like an aura. All this was at least cheerful and even funny, but what I found hard to bear was being kissed in a repetitive way, like a duck at its dinner.

At this point, like the Baker, 'I skip forty years'. It seemed like years, for it was not till eleven o'clock next morning that my first-born appeared. The doctor was very kind; he guessed that I had never had such a long and hard spell of work before. 'Now you understand,' said he, 'the full force of the word "labour".' At this I told him of a German governess I knew who greatly admired the Litany. 'It prays for every one, even the poor governess.' I was puzzled, and asked which petition she meant. 'For all women labouring of child,' she replied. (By the way, it was this linguist who thought that 'Keep to the left' on our street shelters meant 'Asylum for those left behind'.)

Perhaps there may be some greater peaks of happiness for mortals, but I have not heard of anything that could come up to the joy of that morning. It compensated to overflowing for all the trials and difficulties of our ten long years of waiting. And it was a girl that Arthur had been secretly longing for. How swiftly and quietly he came along the passage, afraid to shout or laugh or touch or come too near . . . putting all his energy into rubbing his hands and gazing at this marvel. The babies I had so far seen were little wrinkled, crumpled things, dull red all over, but this was a lovely creature, pink and white, and smooth as a shell. I remembered how my mother used to describe her astonishment at the beautiful face of her second boy—quite unlike the others of us; so I concluded that this vision might actually be my own child and not some heavenly changeling.

Arthur had much difficulty in tearing himself away to the Temple, but got home 'brave and early', as the Cornish say. 'We had a celebration,' said he, 'champagne at the "Cock"; and I've been sending telegrams like mad. And I've put a notice in *The Times*. Atkin advised this, for he says you get more than the money's-worth in gifts from advertising firms.'

And so we did. To Emma's delight every post for several days brought some exotic soap or baby-powder, some patent food or delicate ointment, and a photographer sent us even a photograph of the notice in the paper.

Arthur was so wrapped up in his daughter that his friends in the Temple teased him a little, and accused him once (to his shameless delight) of carrying a bottle of milk in his brief-bag. 'Of course I do,' he replied, 'one mustn't be unprepared, one never knows, and I have a serious job on—I'm founding a dynasty.' One evening as he was brooding over his new possession he said, 'You know I shall be fined for this?' And he explained that when they were on circuit any man who had had a stroke of luck was always fined; there were other strange old customs—for instance, at dinner during his first circuit he was asked which he would have, Old Testament or New. Not knowing what it meant he said, 'Old', as it sounded more solid. And so it was, for he had to drink right off a tumblerful of port. The New would have been only claret. As for the impending fine, I suggested that he shouldn't mention his daughter at all. 'A sound piece of advice,' said he, and laughed.

It was a grand time for me. My room was gay with violets and daffodils, letters of congratulation poured upon me, as well as presents of food dainties, little garments, cot accessories, and so on. My brothers, Tom and Dym, were vociferous in their pleasure at my having achieved a 'lil maid' (to quote Tom's Cornish term of endearment). Neither Arthur nor I had a sister, and my brothers' children were all boys, so that a girl in the family was something of an event. A letter that I valued very much came from Mrs. Ruck, of Pantlludw; after hearty congratulations she added: 'Ask Arthur to repeat to you a Welsh proverb which says, "It's wise in having children to have a girl first."' She ended with a strong wish to hear the new friend's name as soon as it was settled.

'Well, what about her name?' said Arthur as we read this, for we hadn't discussed the matter at all.

'She is Welsh,' said I, 'and there is no doubt what her name must be. She is Bronwen.'

'Do you really mean that?' exclaimed Arthur, glowing with pleasure. The name of his old home in Wales was Fronwen, which means 'the shining hill', and the corresponding name for a girl is Bronwen, which means 'the shining breast'. I felt sure, from the way he used to speak it, that this name made him love her still more.

Among my visitors Yetta was first on the scene, having started immediately on receipt of the telegram. She, too, was delighted at its being a girl, and I believe from the first moment looked upon the little mite as a future student of Bedford College. Yetta was none too satisfied with the nurse, and made some useful alterations in the room and the 'doings' generally. She was a clever nurse herself, leaping to any emergency; in fact she had wanted to take up nursing as a profession, but it had not been considered respectable! She took me for several drives in the Park, as soon as I could be persuaded that the nurse could look after baby in my absence.

Mary Wood was, of course, constantly in and out, providing much comic relief. I saved up for her the nuggets of wisdom that fell from the nurse's lips, as well as her tactful attempts to put me right in points of pronunciation. Thus, for instance, I had said that one of my presents was 'very research' and a few minutes later the word *recherché* was brought casually into the conversation. She was a kindly soul and spared herself no trouble, but oh how glad we were when her month was up, and we could again be by ourselves.

Emma had the country girl's usual wide experience of baby welfare, and was proud to give me the information I required. 'How often should we change her nightdress, Emma?' I asked. The reply was immediate and unequivocal—'Oh, a baby always looks to have a clean one twice a week.' She knew also the odd names for the odd garments that babies wore in that era—such as 'bellyband' (about a yard of flannel that was swathed round and round and safety-pinned on) and 'barracoat' (a garment that I would as easily make as describe).

Naturally in the preceding months I had sought information right and left. My most promising source was Alfred's wife, who had not only a doctor for a husband, but also three children. She took the greatest interest, and loaded me with kindness, but in the matter of what to do about a baby she was, or pretended to be, a blank. 'When I was married,' said she, 'all I knew about a baby was that it had something out of a bottle, and I know little more now. I soon discovered, however, that they are always getting some little thing the matter with them, and then getting quite right again—all on their own. The great thing is that you mustn't fuss about them.' This seemed at the time to be too negative to be useful, but later on I found it by far the most useful bit of advice that I had.

Alfred himself was still more reticent. When Arthur applied to him for advice he said, 'Whatever you do, don't let Molly see a *book* on the subject. They're all useless, and for the most part harmful.' But in spite of this strong negative Arthur couldn't resist buying *Advice to a Wife*, which he found in a remote corner of a railway bookstall. It looked rather weary and second-hand, and if it hadn't been for Arthur's eagle eye for any kind of book it would probably soon have been scrapped. The author was a certain Pye Chevasse, who afforded us merriment if not profit. To him a lady was as delicate as a piece of Venetian glass. She was advised, in the circumstances, to have fresh air in her bedroom (obviously an extreme measure); should the open window be too severe, the door might be left open, and if she were nervous a little chain could be attached to it. Alcohol was not advisable, but she could take her two glasses of port every day with impunity. The chapters were headed with quotations from the Bible, Shakespeare, Spenser, and other worthies, but each was twisted from its original intent; thus, 'Making a sunshine in a shady place' headed a chapter on indigestion. I wish I had kept the book, but Arthur told me to destroy it lest Emma should get hold of it, although there was nothing but its title to excite any one but an antiquary.

Yetta, who provided me with everything she could think of, had arrived one day with a modern book on the subject. This spared nothing in its details of possible disasters (with names for them, too), and I soon saw what Alfred meant by banning books. A chapter headed 'Minor Ailments' provided much amusement for Mary Wood and me. She would burst in with, 'How are you getting on?' and I would reply, 'All right. Only suffering the minor ailments.' One day I had a puzzle for her: 'Look here, Mary, it says in this book, "Have ready for the nurse a pair of blunt scissors." Now my old historical scissors are blunt enough, as you know only too well. But why on earth do they *want* them blunt?' 'They just can't write English,' said Mary, 'they don't mean blunt, they mean rounded at the point, so as not to prick the baby. I'll bring you a pair next time I come.'

When Bronwen was actually on the scene hardly a day went by without a visit from some old friend or relation to greet her. Alfred was now at work in London, and Arthur repeated to me the sympathetic words of this most beloved brother. 'You know, Arthur,' said he, 'when I was first engaged I was brimming with happiness. Then when I was married I knew I was completely happy. But when the first child was born . . . well, I felt that I hadn't known the meaning of the word happy before. So I know all about what you feel.' When he came to see Bronwen he regaled us with a 'turn' he had lately seen: the famous comedian, Arthur Roberts, describing how he had been left for a little while to look after a baby. 'Just keep an eye on it, we shall soon be back,' said its parents. 'Oh, yes, I'll keep an eye on you,' said he to the baby as soon as he was alone with it, 'but nothing shall induce me to pick you up.' 'But,' said he to the audience, 'I picked him up.' 'Well, I've picked you up,' said he to the baby, 'but I'm blowed if I walk about with you.' But he walked about with him. 'I am walking about with you, but I will *not* toss you up and down.' But he tossed him up and down. 'I don't so much mind a little walking and tossing, but nothing on earth shall make me sing to you.' But he sang to him.

All these visits were a great pleasure for me, but what Emma liked best was for us to have Bronwen all to ourselves. What with planning new clothes for her, cutting them out, and creating them, taking her for walks, arranging the cot, going through the ritual of the bath, and preparing dinner in time for Arthur's return, the days flew gaily by, and any little mishap was of no importance at all. One day I was certainly distressed to see my complete stew tilt over into the fire. While I stood looking in dismay at what could not be retrieved, I heard Emma's voice at my elbow, 'Never mind, think of your little Bronwen.' This was apropos of a story I had told her of a small boy who had been given a toy lion— a toy that he lived for. Soon afterwards he was taken to a children's party which had no attractions for him, and he sat gloomy in a corner. Some one looking at him noticed his face suddenly brighten and heard him say, 'I forgot my lion!'

The great moment of the day was seven o'clock, when Arthur was due to come home. There was no music in the world like the sound of his latch-key. His first words never varied when I went to greet him: 'How is she?' Not that there was ever anything the matter with her; but there was always some new accomplishment to relate—a smile, a palpable smile; what *looks* like a tooth coming; an attempt to pull herself up; an enlargement of the appetite; and, of course, an extraordinary intelligence, for which 'taking notice' was a feeble word.

On Saturday afternoons we hoped there would be no visitors or anything at all to disturb Arthur in his complete enjoyment of Bronwen's company. He had bought a kind of weighing machine for recording her progress in pounds and ounces. For this ceremony she was put in one half of my Japanese basket, but it wobbled about so much that I placed no confidence in the weight that was registered. But my arms told me she was getting on.

Yes, Saturday afternoon was the great time for us all. After a short outing, Arthur would settle himself in his deep old basket chair and have Bronwen on his knee. I took my parlour-work and Emma made any excuse she could to hover in and out. Bronwen's idea of sport was to tug her father's moustache till he cried 'Ooh!' Then she took to giving a pro-leptic 'Ooh!' herself, just before a specially hard tug. Toys had been given her in plenty but she took to none of them, sometimes hurling them out of her pram or into her bath. What she liked best was to play with anything that we ourselves were using or wearing. I had brought from Switzerland a brooch with a tiny cow-bell attached, and this she loved to ring. Some optimist had given Arthur a sovereign-purse, which he wore on his watch-chain to inspire confidence; this she would contrive to squeeze into her mouth as she sat on his lap. One afternoon she had become excited with some of these games, and I heard Arthur say, 'Here, Emma, take her; there are ominous sounds.' Ever after that Emma used to refer deli-cately to 'omnibus sounds'. Sometimes Arthur would play a dance tune for her on his fiddle, while she would joggle up and down to it on my lap, and when it came to bed-time he would lull her to sleep with Gwynedd Gwyn. It had for long been his dream to have a daughter who should play the harp, and any pleasure she showed in sounds was a happy omen. Baby-talk he never used to her, but would chat freely to her of this and that, sometimes even appearing to be asking her opinion on some legal point. No doubt he interpreted her gay gurgles quite usefully. One night, in the small hours, she began crying for an extra meal, and continued her demands while I was getting it ready, drawing forth a sleepy protest from Arthur: 'Bronwen, your complaint is not based on the neces-sity of the situation.'

Days were full enough without the need, or desire, for outings of any kind; theatres, concerts, and picture galleries were things of the past for me; and as for Arthur, an occasional dinner in town was all that he indulged in. However, there was to be a great exception. On July 15th, '98, Gray's Inn was to give a ball, the only one (so far as I know) since the jubilee year of 1887. This one, I think, was to celebrate the jubilee of 1897. Arthur said that we must both go.

Gray's Inn had always held a peculiar fascination for me. Arthur had taken me to see the mellow old hall with its oak tables and famous portraits, and told me of the ceremony of the loving-cup on Grand Night, when they toasted 'the pious, glorious, and immortal memory of Good Queen Bess'. On one most memorable occasion, too, I had been permitted to see an actual letter written by Bacon. It was at the time when Arthur and I were greatly interested in the Shakespeare-Bacon controversy, so I looked up at the librarian and said, pointing to the letter, 'Was it this hand that wrote *Hamlet*?' 'That is as you like it,' was the smiling response. The beautiful garden had been another delight—the gateway, the cawing of rooks, the trees and lawns, and especially the old catalpa tree, that was said to have been brought as a sapling from America by Raleigh as a present to Bacon. 'Do you think he really brought it?' I asked Arthur. 'Well,' said Arthur, 'if he didn't he ought to have done.'

Prowling about the Inn like this was one thing, but a ball was quite another, and I immediately pleaded the excuse that I couldn't leave Bronwen for so many hours.

'Nonsense,' said Arthur, 'you can see her safely asleep before we start, and surely Emma can be trusted to look after her for once.'

Emma was so excited at the possibility of such a care, and at the idea of having the cot by her own bed-side for once, that it would have been cruel to disappoint her. My next line of defence—insufficiency of outfit—was useless, since my wedding-dress was all ready, even to the white shoes and stockings. I then abandoned myself to the fun of the thing.

There was the usual sport of Arthur struggling into his dress suit, hunting for his studs, and getting his tie right. It always seems to me that men take much longer than we do over such affairs. Then there was the never-fading joy of a drive in a hansom.

Gray's Inn had let itself go. It was a gloriously hot night, and the whole place seemed to me a fairyland of coloured lights and gaily dressed people, as we all danced and wandered into the garden. I knew several of Arthur's barrister friends, and didn't lack partners. But one of them certainly alarmed me. This was Master Lewis Coward, enormously tall, in court dress, and I believe an extremely important man, a Bencher no doubt. I soon forgot my nervousness, for he danced divinely.

§ 2

When August was upon us we had several invitations for the holidays to choose from. My special aunt, Tony, who had received weekly bulletins of the child's progress, was longing to see her playing about where her grandmother had played. Then Arthur's mother badly wanted her little grand-child. As on many another occasion I was torn between Corn-wall and Wales, but decided on Wales, for I could see that Arthur was dying to show his possession to his people. No sooner had we settled on this than Yetta bore down upon us, and insisted on our going for a fortnight to a farm-house in Brecknock. Indeed she had taken the rooms, and would not hear of a refusal. As she rightly pointed out, it would be a shorter journey than to North Wales. So we agreed to go there first, then on to Aberdovey, leaving the visit to Reska-dinnick till the following year, when Bronwen would be able to run about in its spacious grounds.

Emma was to go 'down hoom' while we were away, and was quite able to see herself off. I gave her an addressed postcard to let me know that all was well. It came, bearing the simple message "rived safe'. Our journey to Hay went off finely, and we were driven in the market cart up to Noyaddu farm, high among the hills. As Yetta had designed, it was a complete holiday for me, and a glorious change for us all after living in a flat. Oats were being carried, wheat being reaped, fowls and ducks and geese continually having something done for them, vegetables, milk, cream, eggs . . . everything in plenty around us. We had drives among the 'Begwns' where we had lovely views of the Black Mountains, or short walks about the fields. Arthur had a day's fishing in the Wye, and brought home twenty-four trout and perch (caught with cock-a-bonddu and hazel fly); so we had trout for supper and perch for breakfast.

Bronwen made rapid advance in weight and length (which we now called height, since she could pull herself upright). But it is her human surroundings that are most vivid in my memory. M'Jane and Yetta had not even a nephew or niece to spend their affection upon, and let it all pour forth on Bronwen. Yetta made garments for her, and M'Jane played baby games with her. The farm was run by a young man and his two sisters, and their aged mother sat in the chimney-corner of the kitchen, too old for work, but not too old to play with Bronwen. I think for her it was a kind of renewal of life as she joined M'Jane in games of peep-bo, pat-a-cake, and blerum. This last performance never never fails to charm a baby. It is done by pouting the lips and flicking the finger up and down them rapidly, at the same time emitting a bubbling sound. Arthur had discovered this in pursuing his hobby of studying old Welsh poetry. A very early poet, named Taliessin, was found (like Moses and Romulus) in the water, and when rescued burst forth into poetry—although he was too much of a baby to be expected even to speak! He was clearly inspired! It was a miracle! A large number of wise bards were assembled, so that they might listen to his wisdom. They sat round the baby in a solemn circle, but all he did was to play blerum at them. It is of course a long story, but that is the short of it.

It was like parting with their own flesh and blood when M'Jane and Yetta said good-bye to Bronwen. We had a queer cross-country railway journey from Hay to Aberdovey, involving a change at Moat Lane, but Bronwen appeared to delight in it all, and was received with rapture by her grandmother. This was not her first grandchild, but it was the first that she was allowed to have all to herself, without any intervening nurse. She had had plenty of sorrow in her life, and in my long acquaintance with her I never knew her so genuinely happy as when she was riding Bronwen on her foot or lap, and singing strange baby doggerel to her. Verses long forgotten came back as soon as she had the child to say them to.

Betsy Brig had a pig, and it was double-jointed;
She tried to make it dance a jig, and she was disappointed.

At such quips Bronwen would laugh as though she saw the joke.

After much searching of the village we managed to hire a mail-cart, and with this we had triumphal walks through the one long straggling street of Aberdovey, where everybody knew us and came up to congratulate and admire. Since this street was open throughout its length to the sea, and faced south, Bronwen thrived faster than ever with the air and the sunshine. She had to be taken, too, by the toy railway up the valley to Aberllefeni, where endless friends and distant relations found striking likeness to her grandfather Hughes. In my heart I detected a likeness to her grandfather Thomas and her uncle Barnholt, whose sunny faces, always fresh in my memory, I longed to see living again.

We returned to London in grand style. Alfred's wife and three children with their nurse had been staying at Aberdovey, and a first-class carriage was engaged for us all. At Euston Alfred was there to meet his people, and Yetta to help us back to Ladbroke Grove. Emma had returned and done all she could think of to make the flat look cosy.

Arthur and I always managed some little celebration for October 2nd, our common birthday. This year we decided to keep it on the preceding Saturday afternoon. We took Bronwen in her pram to browse among the shop-windows of

Notting Hill Gate. We got much pleasure from selecting all the articles of furniture and comforts for the home that it would be good to have, and still more satisfactory to do without. The only shop that it was difficult to get Arthur past was a combination of old curiosities and second-hand books. After enormous deliberation we actually set foot inside this shop. At least, Arthur did, while I stayed outside with Bronwen. I glimpsed him through the doorway as he examined in his short-sighted way pretty well everything on sale. At last he came out with a pair of brass candle-sticks.

'One each for us,' said I, 'and now what for Bronwen?'

'I've got an idea for her,' said Arthur, 'you see I have so little of her company, that I think it would be jolly if she could be more on a level with us at breakfast. Let's buy her a high chair.'

This was a tremendous success. The chair put her on a level with us physically, and almost mentally, for as Arthur read out bits from the paper she would bang with her spoon on the front tray in disapproval, or laugh with approval. And the chair could be let down to a lower level during the day, and seemed safer in this position; but for the most part Bronwen preferred to crawl about and make her own discoveries. As I sat and watched her it occurred to me that I might as well make studies of her little curly toes and rounded legs and arms. These I could do fairly well after my assiduous copying from the old masters in the National Gallery. Then a bolder scheme rose in my mind. I hunted up my old sketch-books and saw that I could make a complete life of Christ in pictures, with the corresponding words from the Gospels underneath, and appropriate poetry from Milton, Herbert, Blake, Keble, and so on, to face them on the opposite page. It was all to be done in proper script, with illuminated capitals and borders, like a medieval manuscript. (Later on Ursula Wood and I carried out this idea together and got it published.)

When Christmas came our difficulty lay in consuming all the good things sent us. As usually happens, our friends were also being overloaded. However, M'Jane and Yetta came to

the rescue and agreed to come to dinner with us on Christmas
Eve and help us eat an enormous turkey sent by Mr. Corner
and reared at his own place. We could not say of it what the
Cornish miner said of a goose—'The worst of it is that it's too
much for one, and not enough for two.' So enormous was it
that none of our pans would hold it, and Arthur and I had to
dash out into Portobello Lane to buy an outsize pan. Time
was of the essence, for it was going to take hours to cook. Our
next trouble was to get it into the oven, but with some bending
and squeezing we managed this at last. It turned out beautifully, and our only regret was that our visitors' appetites had
very little effect on its size. They invited us to pay a return
visit on Boxing Day. Some kind of high chair had been contrived for Bronwen, and she sat up to dinner and behaved
beautifully. In the afternoon the grand drawing-room was at
her disposal to crawl about as she liked; nothing was too
sacred for her to handle and roll about. For a surprise at tea-
time the two sisters had decorated a small Christmas-tree,
with tiny gifts for Bronwen hung about it, and some candles
(placed very safely) and bright-coloured balls among the
branches. They were amply rewarded for their trouble by her
ecstatic little cooings and laughter and thumps on the table.

Among our visitors that winter was Mrs. Keyes. Arthur
came across her one day in Gray's Inn, and told her, of course,
about Bronwen, and invited her to come over to see us. 'Come
to tea next Saturday, and bring your husband.' A child is such
a solvent of social difficulties that Mrs. Keyes was obviously
quite at home as soon as she had Bronwen on her lap. She
declared (and she could have said nothing more warming)
that Bronwen was the living image of Mr. Barnholt. Her husband was too nervous to say much and confined his few
remarks to admiration of the flat. As they were going he put
a hand lovingly on the dark-brown dado of the passage.
Drawing me aside he said in a low tone : 'The best of this, you
see, Mum, is when you come home a bit late and that, and
you lean against the wall, it doesn't show the mark.' How
Arthur and I used to laugh afterwards about the uses of our

dado. I am pleased at the memory of that visit, for not many months later we heard that both Mrs. Keyes and her husband were ill. I went to see them in their room in one of those depressing model dwellings somewhere off Gray's Inn Road. The few comforts I had taken were nothing for people needing regular nursing, and I felt wretched and helpless about them, till in walked a Roman Catholic nun, and 'took hold'. 'It's all right,' said she, 'we come in twice a day and do all that is possible for them.' But she told me outside the door that there was no hope that either of them would live.

My dear old friend of college and 'bachelor diggings' time, Miss Rogers, made a pilgrimage to see me, bringing a quilt for the cot, made by herself. She expected to find me sobered into the staid married woman, and on her entrance behaved accordingly. But her wonted address soon burst out: 'Molly, you owl, you are making your poor infant as full of senseless laughter as yourself. Here, give her to me.' Whereupon Bronwen was promptly deposited on Miss Rogers's lap and taught sillier games than even I had indulged in.

Not a week passed without a visit from Mary Wood, my friend in every phase of life. 'How I wish you would be married, too,' I often said to her, and she as often replied, 'Find me a man exactly like Arthur, and I'll marry him at once.' She dropped in at any hour, and shared in any meal. Bronwen seemed almost her own child, and as godmother she used to ask frequently, 'When shall I step in with the ten commandments?' Her eldest sister and her husband were treated with rather more ceremony and asked to dinner in a proper way now and again. Such visits were always heartily enjoyed, but after one of them I noticed Arthur looking annoyed and fretful. This was so unusual that I said, 'What's the matter? Dinner all right, wasn't it?' 'Yes, everything went splendidly.' 'Well, then?' 'Oh I'm so ashamed,' said he, with a scowl, 'when people who have no child come here and see me with Bronwen.' I was astounded. 'But surely you're not ashamed of being seen with her on your knee?' 'Gracious, no. But I feel that I have had far more than my share—everything in life that I've most wanted. I feel when any one childless comes here just as ashamed as a millionaire ought to be when he shows off his house to a chap who lives in a hovel.'

These particular guests were, I believe, perfectly happy in their life of painting, and needed no commiseration. But one of our visitors seemed to have endured far more than her share of the blows of fate. A career of sin or crime, romantic struggles with poverty, a pathetic illness—any such excitements would have been better than my Aunt Lizzie's meek endurance of a miserable married life and lonely widowhood. Perhaps her lack of endearing foibles was her most serious shortcoming. Her religion must have given her consolation; but it's a poor religion that adds no gaiety. The fact is that when she proposed to spend a fortnight with us I was a little alarmed at the idea, dreading a criticism of my domestic methods, or lack of them. When Bronwen was born she had written to me, 'Is not your heart singing with joy all day long?' Even this remark, astonishing from her, didn't make me aware of all the empty longing she must have endured. But when she came my eyes were opened. To me she seemed some one absolutely new. I never remember to have heard her laugh before, and now, as she tended Bronwen, complete bliss shone in her face. We had merry shoppings in Portobello Lane. Aunt Lizzie was trusted to wheel the pram and even to do the bathing and dressing. Bronwen would sit contentedly in her lap, exploring her watch-chain and brooch and buttons, looking up into her face with laughter at each fresh discovery. Having the child in her arms aroused old memories of her visits to us when we were children, and she regaled me with many an anecdote about my brothers: how little Tom, when only three, on hearing talk of an outing, managed to pull open a big drawer and drag out his best velvet suit; how she saved the new-born Charles's life when he was all but dead, and no doctor at hand; how little Barnholt greeted her once with urgent whisperings of 'Appoo pooun—appoo pooun' (interpreted by his mother as the glad news that there was to be apple pudding for dinner).

Another thing that we enjoyed together was the planning and preparing the dinner for the evening. Aunt Lizzie had had long experience both in choosing the best joints and vege-tables to buy, as well as in the most appetizing ways to cook them. She knew sixteen different ways of doing potatoes, and how to make a proper Irish stew and a real curry. She was delighted at my eagerness in writing down all her hints in my manuscript cookery book.

Shortly before she arrived she had sent us her piano. She had now given up her teaching and said she no longer needed it. It was a grand acquisition for us, as I was able to practise again and accompany Arthur on his violin. Why is it that we are always more grateful for what people take from us than for what they give us? That piano is still with me and is a continual reminder of my aunt; but what I really thank her for is that fortnight in which she took Bronwen to her heart and was made happy.

§ 3

The great event in the spring of 1899 was Bronwen's birth-day. As Arthur was leaving in the morning he gave her a toss in his arms and exclaimed, 'One year old! You are now riding on your two, as the Welsh say.' He promised to be sure to come home for tea.

I was expecting quite a birthday party. Mary Wood was unable to come, but sent a white silk frock for her god-daughter to look grand for the occasion. One of my Cornish cousins and an old college friend came with gifts of shoes. M'Jane and Yetta brought a large ball for Bronwen to roll about, and a blue silk sash to add to her white frock. With them came an old lady friend of theirs and, most valuable of all, a cousin, an eight-year-old boy. This little Wilfred laid aside his dignity, abandoned himself to the situation, and crawled about the floor with Bronwen. He not only chased the ball with her as though it were the one end in life, but also he made circles with his arms and arches with his legs for her to crawl through to reach the ball, which she managed with crows of triumph.

This was my first serious tea-party, and it seemed quite a cheerful company with no lack of conversation. On the material side I had endeavoured to make it as grand as possible, with wedding-presents at last given a chance to be shown off. On a wooden tray, carved for me by Miss Russell, the secretary of Bedford College, I had laid out the blue tea-service given me by M'Jane. A home-made cake, and some more reliable bought ones, I had displayed on a table given me by Mrs. Bryant. These various objects provided more talk when it was most required, for one of the wedding-presents was creating a hold-up; this was an extremely ornamental brass kettle on a tall tripod stand, with a minute methylated spirit-lamp poised in the middle. It was the first occasion that had been important enough for its use, and I may add that it was the last. However, it had one advantage—it afforded great pleasure to Yetta, who knew exactly how to manage it, and took over the duty. Even under her control it looked like being a long time before the thing would actually come to the boil, so I slid out into the kitchen to engineer a preliminary pot of tea in order to set things going. Here I found Emma in a great state of agitation. I had sent her out to get some cream at a dairy close by. 'Look mum,' she cried, 'what they've charged me a shilling for! Why, down hoom it would have been tuppence.'

The tea was poured out and cream added when Arthur breezed in, just in time to help Wilfred hand round the things. He felt obliged to remark that the birthday cake was a bit sad in the middle, but M'Jane immediately insisted that the best cakes are always sad in the middle. She also remarked when Bronwen's white silk frock showed signs of devaluation from the floor exercise, 'Never mind, Molly, it will wash like a rag.' One would like to have M'Jane behind one at the Day of Judgement.

After this first milestone Bronwen forged ahead faster than ever. She could walk about by pushing a little chair in front of her. She would spring in my arms with gleeful cries of

'Mum, Mum', and welcome her father with 'Dad, Dad'. Her favourite word was 'up', the most expressive, I suppose, in the whole language, for joy or sorrow, life or death—we wake up and we break up. Often I heard Bronwen muttering it softly to herself before attempting the adventure; then she would pull herself upright to chair or couch and exclaim aloud 'Up', as triumphant as one who has achieved the Matterhorn.

Mary Wood's sister Ursula was then specializing in portraits, and suggested that she should do an oil-colour of Bronwen sitting in her high chair. This idea was particularly pleasing to Arthur, for his main vision of her was the little person thus seated at breakfast, 'chatting' to him in her own way. The portrait was a big business, necessitating several visits, and I wondered how Ursula managed it at all, for a lively baby can't pose, and has to be caught; but it turned out a great success.

The last days of May were upon us, and the warm spring sunshine was penetrating the flat, making us think of the coming summer and our long-promised visit to Cornwall, when we could show Bronwen to Tony, who would be sure to spoil her as she had spoilt all of us.

One evening my old headmistress and friend, Miss Bennett, came over to see us. Whether it was the effect of the baby or not I can't say, but she seemed to have shed her extreme propriety and to be as humanly foolish as our other visitors. She pronounced Bronwen to be the picture of health, and I said, 'She has not had an hour's illness since she was born.' It was pleasant to note that Miss Bennett lapsed, as we all do at times, into our ancient paganism. 'Oh, don't say that,' she immediately rejoined, 'you know how the Greeks felt that the gods are jealous of human happiness, and if they hear people boasting . . .' She broke off with a merry laugh and shake of the head.

It was two mornings later that I noticed a new accomplishment in the little creature lying in her cot by my side. She was gurgling to herself, and waving her little hands about, as though keeping time to some tune she had made. As I watched, the sounds changed to something like a moan, and I soothed her to sleep in my arms. We were troubled to see that she hadn't her usual appetite for breakfast, and made no objection to being laid in her cot again. Arthur was distressed out of all proportion to such a slight indisposition; said he had a case in court or would stop at home; he would look in at the doctor's as he went by, to send him along; and I must be sure to send a wire if things were the least bit worse.

The doctor came at once, and thought there was a little stomach trouble; I was to give no food, but watch very carefully and send for him again if things didn't improve. I kept her in my arms all day, and she slept a little and smiled now and again, so that I felt hopeful that the trouble was passing. But at about four o'clock, when I thought she might swallow a little warm milk, she suddenly threw back her little head and began to gasp, and then to my horror she became unconscious. I told Emma to fetch the doctor, and then to go on to the post office and wire to the Temple, 'Come home as early as you can'. I made her repeat the message very carefully. There was no need to tell the poor girl to hurry. Half distracted when alone with the little one I made my way to the book-case, found Yetta's book of advice, and with one hand managed to see what to do in case of a fit—a hot bath was suggested. I went to the kitchen again but could do nothing about it till Emma's return. At last she appeared. The doctor was out, but would come as soon as he returned. In her anxiety she had wired the words to Arthur, 'Come at once'. This added to my anguish, for I knew how such a message would turn his heart to water. I ought to have remembered that whenever he was in a tight place all his wits were quickened, and that he would never spend an ounce of energy in mere emotion that might be useful in action. He did not come at once. Instead of that he tore round to his brother Alfred and brought him along with him. He also wired to Yetta, knowing her to be practical as well as ever ready to help. She was one of the governors of the London Hospital, and she wired for a nurse to be sent to me post-haste.

I pass over hurriedly, although I can recall them only too vividly, the details of those dreadful hours, as the fight for the little life went on. The fit passed off, consciousness returned, and there came the blissful sound, the familiar little 'Mum, Mum'. It was a chance that did redeem all sorrows that ever I had felt.

The doctor and Alfred hung over the cot, with the nurse attending, keeping on with various spongings to keep the temperature down. Arthur and I stood by in the back-ground. After hours of watching Alfred whispered something to Arthur, and I was asked to go and fetch some necessity—I forget what. Only too thankful to be able to do something I went into the dining-room to find the thing required. I had barely got there when Arthur followed me into the room, shut the door, took me in his arms and dropped his head on my shoulder with the words: 'Let her go.'

The supreme phases of our life here—love and birth and death—each has the power of breaking down the barrier between us. We glory in the first two, in spite of their attendant pain. Why don't we acknowledge the majestic strength of the last? In that moment of anguish Arthur and I were one as we had never been before. But our poor human frames crack under the pain, and I hope I may never again see a man broken down with grief.

Since writing this short record I have realized the number of empty hearts that Bronwen filled with warmth and joy. And she did her little stroke all unawares . . . 'dear childe'.

XIII

Three Sons

D URING the following years three boys came to cheer us.
Our natural anxiety about the health of the first gradually lessened as he got over every little ailment, and
when his two brothers grew strong and lively our cares were
thrown to the winds.

Life was so full of things to be done every moment that there
was hardly room for worry to take root. Money was never
plentiful, and we were glad to add a little to our coffer by some
simple literary work. Through Mr. Corner's influence Arthur
was given the job of writing the London Letter for the *Here-
fordshire Times* once a week. I was proud to be able to contri-
bute a paragraph to this now and again, and I also wrote an
occasional article for an educational paper, and did a great
many reviews. All this made a pleasant change from domestic
duties. I can give no orderly account of those strenuous years,
but pull from my memory a few happenings that stand out,
not for their importance, but for some oddity.

Londoners who live in flats are more distant with one
another, if that is possible, than next-door neighbours. This
is, no doubt, from the fear that the proximity would be un-
bearable if relations became at all strained. In the flat below
us there came to live a young married couple, and after a while
I ventured to call. I was well received, and as we chatted I
learnt that a baby was expected. I immediately offered to lend
the trestle-bed I had bought for my nurse, and a few other
appurtenances that were now lying idle. At this the lady drew
herself up and looked at me queerly, obviously suspecting me
of some sinister motive. 'But,' said she, 'why should you, a
perfect stranger, lend me these things?' I replied that I was an
old Londoner and knew that such an offer from a neighbour
was *ultra vires*, but that I was also a Cornish woman, and accus-

tomed to a different code. Then we both laughed and became friends. So much so indeed that later on, when she was in difficulties after her nurse had left, I was actually allowed to go down and bath the baby for her. She little knew what delight it was to me to have such a task again.

That friendship was the only *rapprochement* afforded by the neighbourhood as such. We had endless visits from old friends, from relations passing through London, from my old schoolfellows, and from any friends of theirs who were within hail. But from mere neighbours, not one. There were several churches close by, but no clergyman called on us. People in flats are regarded as birds of passage, no doubt, devoid of souls, although we stayed seven years, and strange to say my friend below is still in her flat with husband and daughter.

One child in a flat is all right, but when we had two boys we felt that more space was wanted, and a bit of garden. We consulted Bradshaw to find some spot that was 'country' and yet provided with a few fast trains to town. Barnet filled the bill, and was specially attractive to me for its associations with my father and brothers, who used to take long walks from it as a base. The very name pleased me, as reminiscent of my brother Barnholt.

In those days Barnet was very different from what it is to-day. There were no trams, and the only bus was a little one-horse affair that plied between New and High Barnet—continually to be seen, but never on the spot when wanted. Where now you see road after road of new prim villas, of latest design, we enjoyed spacious open fields, country lanes, with over-hanging hedges, and enticing foot-paths. Our house was an old one, overlooking a park with a large pond and great spreading trees. A gate at the bottom of our garden led into the grounds of our landlord, a kindly old fellow who loved the company of one of our small boys as he pottered among his fruit trees and vegetables.

Kindly, yes, and so was every one else. Accustomed all my life to the aloofness of Londoners I was amazed at the immediate friendliness of the Barnet people. The vicar came quite soon, and of course a doctor was necessary when our third boy arrived. Both the vicar's wife and the doctor's wife were of that charmingly indiscreet type that is the despair of their husbands and the joy of their neighbours.

Another rich vein of friendship was the railway journey to town. Arthur was soon one of a coterie who took the same express every morning. He went third-class, but it was soon usual for some of the richer business men to forsake their first-class carriage and join those whose purses were lighter and conversation brighter.

What with the vicar and the doctor, our quite contingent neighbours, and the wives of Arthur's train companions, I soon had plenty of friends. Paying calls, however, was not in my line, and I found it expedient to build up a character for eccentricity.

'You promised to come and see me,' said a friend I met in the road, 'but you have never been.'

'Ah,' said I, 'but then I never meant what I said. What I like is for people to drop in on me just when they feel inclined and never expect me to call on them.'

She was too astonished to be offended, and fell in pleasantly with the idea. So did many others, and hardly a day passed without some one popping in, to exchange notes about a cookery recipe, to play with the boys, or join in with anything we were doing.

The days were full enough, for although I had a servant for housework I never had a nurse. This was not so much from lack of means as from my preference for looking after the boys myself. There was no kindergarten at hand, and even if there had been one I should not have cared to send them to it. Kindergartens are fine institutions, but those I had seen gave me the impression of too much dainty attention to the children, too much absorption in their important work on the part of the teachers, too much of the 'Isn't he sweet?' and 'Isn't she a darling?' My ideal was more of a rough-and-tumble environment. A married servant of my mother's said to her once, in solemn tones, 'You know, mum, children *thrive* in the dirt.' Mother perceived the big principle underlying this statement, and determined that her own children should be perfectly clean once a day, and beyond that might get as dirty as they liked.

Our new surroundings were splendid for such an ideal. There was an attic at the top of the house for the boys' own, to set out their train lines, build with their bricks, and romp as they liked. There was a garden to grub in and trees to climb. I didn't want to make them nervous, and I hope it will be counted to me for righteousness that when I heard a 'Hullo, mother!' from the top branches of the fir, or saw a boy walking along the perilous edge of the garden wall, I went indoors to suffer in silence, often muttering to myself Hagar's 'Let me not see the child die'.

Not far away was a pond, containing minnows and stickle-backs, and one afternoon a little figure appeared slung about with every appliance for catching them and a glass jar for bringing them home. 'I'm going fishing, mother,' he announced. 'Won't you have your tea before you go?' I asked. 'No; fishermen do not care to eat.' The right spirit, I thought.

Casualties were frequent to both bodies and garments, but nothing serious. Falls downstairs, grazed knees, cut fingers, and bruises were little accounted of. A great triangular tear in knickerbockers would be shown me, with 'It won-matter, will it, mother? It'll soon mend, won't it?' In such a case as this I found one of my neighbourly visitors extremely useful. 'Oh, do let me mend it, Mrs. Hughes,' and of course I hadn't the heart to refuse her.

Materials of all kinds were in constant demand for operations in the attic. String, empty bobbins, pieces of wood, bits of cloth, sheets of brown paper—but commonest of all was the query, 'Have you got a box, mother?' 'What size do you want?' 'Oh, just a box.' I have not yet cured myself of hoarding every box that comes to the house.

Naturally I tried to give the boys some serious teaching, and soon found that very little actual sitting down to it was required. At least on my part. Each boy, after reaching the responsible age of four, was set down to some morning task. But any reasonable outside demand was permitted. Thus, one morning the second boy was a very long time coming home after seeing his father off at the station. 'Where have you been?' said I, for he looked rather the worse for wear, although radiant. 'I been delivering with Payne,' was the proud reply. Payne was our greengrocer, and the little chap had been staggering to people's doors with greens and potatoes. I guessed that he had learnt as much in that way as in his 'lessons' at home.

These lessons chiefly consisted in the boys doing something by themselves while I was busy in the kitchen. Results or difficulties were brought to me wherever I happened to be. Drawing of some kind was the basis of nearly everything. Thus for starting reading I had made a packet of cards, drawn an object on each and printed its name below; so the word (as it would look in a book) became familiar long before the separate letters were distinguished. Then it could be copied, and there was the beginning of writing. The transition to real reading was made easy through Mary Wood, who brought something to help me every time she came. Among her gifts were two books of priceless value. The story of *Little Black Sambo* was read aloud to the boys, soon known by heart, acted in the garden, and then read by themselves—such words as 'beautiful' and 'umbrella' (impossible to teach on any rational system) being soon recognized in any context. The other book was a little folk's edition of *Alice in Wonderland*. By the time that these, and *Peter Rabbit*, were mastered there was no more anxious bother about reading. I have seen countless books of 'systems' for teaching children to read, and have come to the conclusion that the only thing is to give them a book (with some good illustrations) containing a story that they *want* to know.

In spite of Mr. Harding's warning I followed his ideas about the beginnings of arithmetic. With the boys' assistance I painted red spots on postcards, arranged as on playing-cards, so that a five, a six, a seven, and so on could be quickly intuited.

A few of these would be dealt out and added up, such words as twenty, thirty, and forty coming as happily surprising new words. One day the glad news was reported to me in the kitchen, 'Mother, I've got to *tenty*!' That was the moment to acquire the new word 'hundred'.

Quite another aid to realizing number and size came in an unexpected way. The gift of a very large box of plain bricks gave endless pleasure for building purposes. The well-made pieces of hard wood varied in size from a cubic inch to lengths of ten inches, adapting themselves to being railway lines or men-of-war with rising decks or houses or temples, while the little cubes could pose as people. It was only as I watched the play that I perceived their further value. 'Hand me a six,' one busy builder would cry. 'Can't find a six, will a four and a two do?' The actual handling of the different sizes seemed to me valuable, and I encouraged a pride in putting all the bricks in the box before bed, for the mere fitting in had its advantages. The boys are now scattered far and wide, but those bricks are still intact.

I don't know whether the love of measurement is common in children, but the boys seemed to have a passion for it, and the eldest enjoyed even angles and the use of a protractor. I told him one day to draw any number of triangles he liked, all shapes and sizes; then to measure the angles in each very carefully and to add the results. I went about my own business, and after a long time came the surprised report: 'It's so funny, mother, they all come out the same!'

Occasionally it was one of the boys who set a problem to me, and I was not always equal to it. One day I was at the sink washing up the tea-things, when the youngest approached with, 'Mother, who *is* the Holy Ghost?' I confess that I temporized: 'I'm busy just now, darling, but another time. . . .' He ran off contented and forgot his difficulty. Another day the middle boy, chancing to be out with me alone, asked me what electricity was. Here I felt on surer ground, and enlarged on the subject at some length, not a little pleased at the silent attention of my audience. I was rewarded with, 'Oh well, when Dad comes home I'll ask him, and he'll splain it properly.'

Arthur had plenty of explanations to make, for my know-ledge of mathematics or engineering was never regarded as reliable. It was the early days of motor-cars, and they were rare enough for us to make a game of counting them on the Great North road; one boy kept a little note-book for recording their numbers. On one grand afternoon we had the bliss of seeing King Edward go by. On another hardly less exciting occasion we saw an aeroplane over our fields for the first time. It used to delight me to see Arthur with one boy on his knee, and the other two hanging on his shoulders, while he drew diagrams and explained what the inside of a locomotive was busy about, what the different wheels of a watch were for, how a motor-car worked, and how a plane managed to get up.

In the matter of geography I was sketchy, being content with getting the boys to know where important places were, and to be fond of maps. With the aid of picture postcards we got on fairly well. The counties of England and Wales, and the countries of Europe were learnt without trouble by means of puzzles, sensibly made so that each county or country was a separate piece. I would hear, 'What's become of Devon? It's that nice fat one,' or 'Find Northampton for me; it's a long one.' Rutland was troublesome, in constant danger of being lost.

As for grammar I was on velvet. When I had books to review there had fallen into my hands *The Child's Picture Grammar*, a gem by Rosamund Praeger, gloriously illustrated in colour. In most schools there is much agony inflicted on teachers and taught by trying to cope, in junior classes, with case and gender, voice, mood, and tense—many of them things that the English language has wisely thrown off. All that a healthy child needs to know is the business of each part of speech. Now this book depicted them in anthropomorphic style, with comic illustrations and a story, so that they became personal friends of the boys. The page on pronouns showed two boys fighting, while their grown-up nouns were having a rest. They had got confused as to which noun they each represented. In this way the useful slogan was learnt—'One pronoun, one job'.

Our literary efforts were neither exalted in style nor improving in tone. The boys certainly delighted in the poems of Elizabeth Turner and of Jane and Ann Taylor, but not for their moral value. They never tired of the sailor lads of Bristol City, of the Pied Piper, the Jackdaw of Rheims, the Pobble who had no toes, and the Bishop of Rumtifoo. I would hear scraps of these being chanted about the house: 'Blow your pipe there till you burst', 'They were 'educed to one split pea', '*Time*, my Christian friend.' Not but what I tried to instil some verses of deeper value. But it was no use; I saw that it was merely 'filling the kettle with the lid on', and soon learnt how foolish it is to press lovely poems on young people before they can naturally appreciate them, and thus deprive them of the shock of delight that awaits them later on. It is better never to hear a fine piece of literature at all than to hear it with distaste. However, there was one supreme poem that I couldn't resist giving the boys—*The Ancient Mariner*. They enjoyed the mystery and weirdness of the story, and I did not require it to be learnt by heart, but now and again I would hear scraps of it being muttered, such as 'And every soul, it passed me by, like the whizz of my cross-bow'. Last thing before bedtime I used to 'read a chapter' to them. I chose something soporific rather than serious, and it was usually an episode from Uncle Remus, or *Rudder Grange*, or *The Diary of a Pilgrimage*, all of which the boys knew well enough to join in with the story here and there. But I tried to make up the deficiency of more solid stuff in another way.

Unless the weather was absolutely forbidding, every afternoon was spent in a walk. Hadley Woods provided a glorious playground for exploring glades, climbing, jumping, hiding, gathering blackberries, collecting chestnuts, or watching the various kinds of trains going by on the Great Northern. But we had a walk to and from the woods through rather dull streets. The youngest boy was in and out of a mail-cart, and quite content, but the other two were bored on the way out and tired on the way back. So to ease the situation I used to tell stories, on the true Chaucerian model. As may be supposed, I was frequently gravelled for matter. To 'tell a story' in an isolated way is difficult when the demand is continual. A verse of Keats came to my mind—'All lovely tales that we have heard or read, an endless fountain of immortal drink'—I began to explore the various sources of good tales that I knew, and found them indeed endless. To save the bother of selection I assigned a different day to each source: thus, on Mondays I told a Bible story, on Tuesdays a story from English history, on Wednesdays one from Roman history, on Thursdays one from the *Iliad* or *Odyssey*, and on Fridays a fairy story or a Norsk legend or a fable from Aesop. Of course I had to enlarge and embroider to make the stories last out. I remember taking the length of Station Road to describe the gorgeous home of the rich young ruler—his horses, his grand dinners, his purple clothes, his apes and peacocks (these last borrowed from Solomon). The boys saw that it was no light thing to give up all these jolly things to go and help among the very grubby poor people that he could see around Jesus. It was after some such story that the middle boy said, 'What happens to us when we die, mother?' 'Nobody knows,' I replied. 'Ah,' said he, 'I expect Jesus is keeping it secret, so that we shall have a nice little surprise.'

I suppose to children there are few things to equal the pleasure of surprise, especially the surprise of an unopened parcel. Christmas was the grand time for this, when every present was put away until the appointed moment. It was a day or two before this feast when the middle boy said to me, 'I hope you will die on Christmas Day, mother.' 'Well,' said I, 'it's not very likely that I shall, why do you want me to?' 'I want to see the blood coming out.' 'Oh, but you know people often die without the blood coming out, you can't rely on it.' 'Oh well, then, never mind, don't bother about it.'

Of course, the boys had many picture books, and no doubt made up strange stories for themselves from them. Their father arrived one Saturday afternoon with an enormous volume of Hogarth. He had picked it up at a sale and had great trouble in dragging its weight home to the door. It is only when I am in extremely high spirits that I can bear to look at those terrible satires. I was surprised to find how often the youngest boy demanded to have it put on the floor for him, and would apparently revel in it. Idly one day I said, 'Which picture do you like best?' He said at once, 'Oh this one, mother,' and turned to Hogarth's realistic depiction of a man being drawn and quartered.

Home-made picture books provided a useful pastime. I got some blank scrap-books, and the boys pasted into them any odd pictures they could collect. One book was kept for history, another for geography, and another for illustrations of the Bible. All this involved much cutting and messing with gum. The house was never very tidy. One morning a neighbour looked in and expressed astonishment at finding me busily engaged in putting everything to rights. 'I read in the paper yesterday,' said I, 'about a woman who was murdered, and it said that the police found her cupboards and drawers in great disorder. So I thought I had better tidy up a bit, in case I get murdered.' 'Don't you worry,' said my kindly neighbour, 'the drawers will all get untidy again before you are murdered.'

While I was a source of amusement to the people of Barnet, Arthur was a pillar of strength. All sorts of troubles and family difficulties were brought to him, and he never failed to do something or other to help, even if it was only by his calm and sympathetic way of getting to the kernel of the trouble. On one occasion a neighbour's son had got into disgrace, on another a neighbour's daughter had been found dead in a pond, on another a husband's feelings were acutely hurt because his wife (who was known to drink a little in private) had been refused communion. In all these troubles Arthur managed to help in some way. The vicar was a young man, very enthusiastic about introducing high church practices. Some hot-headed protestants became full of righteous indignation, held meetings and 'exposed' his carryings-on in the local press. He walked about the street in cassock and biretta, and was accused of wearing a mitre! Arthur said he neither knew nor cared what the vicar chose to put on, but he would not have him hounded by people who seldom, if ever, entered the church. So he attended one of these indignation meetings, and let his fury have full scope. The effect was almost magical, for what Arthur said *went*. He could never forget the bitterness of the nonconformists in Wales towards the Church schools, and how the children were denied proper equipment and even sufficient coal. 'If I were on the local council there,' he would growl, 'I would get things altered.' 'But what could you do,' I objected, 'if you were the only churchman there?' 'Do? Why, I'd raise hell, and be carried out of every meeting.'

And indeed the objections to our vicar came entirely from the nonconformists in the parish, who, of course, had no interest in the church, but asserted their right as parishioners to fight for the Lord by stopping Romish practices. It was during this local warfare that Tom came to stay with us, and was all agog to see what the practices were like. 'D'you call this high?' he whispered to me in a disgusted tone during the service, 'In Middlesbrough we should call it *low*!'

Tom was a grand companion for the boys, and the youngest sat on his knee whenever possible. When I protested, the little chap maintained that 'there was nowhere else to sit'. This was in a field, where, as Tom said, there were all the home counties to sit in. In church, of course, he had to behave in more seemly fashion and confine his energies to making a train of the hassocks. Tom had given each boy a new sixpence, and one of them had placed it on the pew for happy contemplation through the sermon. When the bag came round Tom made him put the sixpence in, explaining to the agonized child that it must go in because it had been so openly advertised. I think, however, that another one was soon found.

Sunday was never a dull day, for we had Arthur at home for walks or games or reading or singing. Moreover, I instituted a 'Sunday box', never opened except on Sunday. In this I had gradually accumulated a number of diminutive toys, which could be employed in endless combinations. The only one who loathed Sunday was our Welsh terrier, who used to lie down in limp dejection when he heard the church bell; but he cheered up in the afternoon when a long walk over the fields to Cockfosters gave him glorious chances of getting as muddy as he liked.

We never pressed any religious instruction on the boys, merely answering their questions as sincerely as we could, as they arose. I had always felt the truth of Jean Paul Richter's remark that children imbibe religion best by noting their parent's attitude to it—no matter what is taught or preached in church. I sometimes wondered what the boys made of the curious prayers and hymns and sermons, but said nothing. Once when the Athanasian Creed was being intoned I observed the youngest boy following intently with his book. Presently he pulled me down to whisper in my ear, 'Mother, what awful rubbish this is.'

The religious occasion that we most enjoyed was the Welsh service at St. Paul's on the eve of St. David's Day. Arthur was on the committee for organizing it, and so we always had good reserved seats. The cathedral was packed to overflowing by people who had come up from Wales on purpose for it. The band of the Welsh Guards led the music, and the singing of *Hen Wlad Fy Nhadau* (which the Dean and Chapter probably thought was a hymn) was the most tremendous thing I have ever heard. The whole service and the sermon were in Welsh, conducted by Welsh clergymen from various parts. But the cathedral vastness needs some management, so the final blessing delivered from the distance of the altar was entrusted to one of the canons, coached up in the Welsh for the occasion. Arthur had been busy over arrangements for this festival when he died—a few days before. I was told that they played the Dead March in *Saul*.

Long years ago Arthur had confided to me his secret ambition to get into Parliament. We both knew that our limited means would forbid it for ages, and probably for ever.

Imagine my excitement, therefore, when one evening he came 'home with the news that he was to fight Lloyd George at the coming election. 'Mind you,' said he, 'there's not the ghost of a chance that I shall get in.' 'Never mind,' said I, 'you will have the fight. But why do they trouble to put up a candidate when it's hopeless?' 'Because if there was no opposition, Lloyd George would be free to go about supporting other candidates. It's worth the money to the party merely to keep him out of action.'

And a grand time we all had. Arthur was provided with a car and a chauffeur (a luxury in those days) and was driven about the Division at hot speed from one meeting to another. Every morning came a letter from him about hecklings and even escapes from physical attacks, and when the elections began we became very busy at home. We had a large map of England spread out on the table, and whenever a result was published we stuck a little flag in the place—bits of red and blue paper on pins. Moreover, we decorated the mail-cart with flags and made a brave show through the streets of Barnet. Some of our many friends were of the opposite colour, which added piquancy to our encounters. Of course Arthur was defeated, but he had successfully kept Lloyd George on the hop, and this had given him immense satisfaction.

Not long after this it was my turn to have a jaunt from home. An advertisement of excursions on the Great Western caught my eye. One could go to Penzance and back for fifteen shillings. I had never been in an excursion train in my life, and believed them to be all that was miserable and degrading. Still—only fifteen shillings for a chance to see Cornwall once again, and Tony. I asked Arthur what he thought about it. He immediately wanted me to travel properly by the ordinary train. But I pointed out that I couldn't leave the boys for more than two nights, and that it would be great fun to see what an excursion was like, and that anyhow I would go like that or not at all. Strange to say, it was the easiest journey to Cornwall I ever had. Arthur saw me off from Paddington at 8 p.m.; there were only two other passengers in my compartment and I went immediately to sleep. 'Where are we?' said I when I woke. 'Newton Abbot,' was the reply.

With what rapture I took that early morning walk from Camborne station down to Reskadinnick. Every turn of the road brought to mind some jolly incident of my childhood, some dearly loved person. As I went along the drive, where every tree seemed an old friend, I had again that uncanny feeling of being uncertain that my surroundings were real, or that I had any business there—just as I had felt when alone in New York. The house at last! The same as ever. I went round by the side way, through into the poultry yard, and there by a hen-coop, leaning upon her stick, stood Tony. I stopped, and she looked at me in a dazed way, and then exclaimed, 'Why! 'tis Molly!'

When I see cheap excursions advertised on posters I often wonder whether they are going to provide people who are hard up with some such golden opportunity as I had—a chance to see some one whom they will never see again. The bliss of that day to Tony and me is indescribable. I followed her about as I did when a child, helped her with little jobs, or just sat with her and talked. I made her go to bed early and brought up her supper to her.

'Arthur has sent you a little medicine for your rheumatism,' said I, as I took from my bag a large-size medicine bottle, 'and it's got to be taken in hot water, and lemon and sugar may be added. I've brought up a kettle and everything.'

'Dear Arthur!' said she, 'how good of him, and I feel to want some quite at once.'

As she sipped it lovingly I told her that it was part of a gift of superb whisky given to Arthur by a grateful client.

For as far back as I can remember it had been her custom to read a psalm at bed-time. A large-print volume of them lay by her side. Never did she stray into the rosy paths of the New Testament, but found a companion for every mood, from gaiety to black despair, in her 'royal treasury' of the Psalms.

'Which one shall I read to you to-night?' said I, picking up the book.

'Well, it isn't its turn, dear, but do let's have the hundred and fourth. I love to think of God feeding all the creatures, the wild asses quenching their thirst and the lions roaring after their prey.'

'I believe you know it by heart,' said I. She nodded and smiled, and before I had reached the verse about the lions she was peacefully asleep.

The next morning I had to start very early, but she was up to give me breakfast, and my last memory of her is that brave figure, crippled by age and rheumatism, standing in the garden to wave a last farewell to me as I turned the bend into the drive.

On my reaching home, I found that the boys had had a good time in the servant's care, and that Arthur had been adequately fed. When I recounted my unnecessary anxiety to Mrs. Macbeth, a neighbour with boys of her own, she told me how she had learnt not to worry: 'When Ronald was four years old I had to go to town for the day, and, of course, I left full instructions for his care—fire to be guarded—no going near the pond—no window to be open at the bottom—you know the sort of thing. But while I was in full career of shopping a cold fear seized me—what if Ronald should go playing with the mangle and crush his finger? So I hunted for a post office (no easy thing in London!) and telegraphed home, "Keep Ronald from mangle", and then went back to my shopping with complete peace of mind. When the door was opened on my return I was told that everything was all right, but that there was a telegram for me. Like an idiot, I had addressed it "Macbeth", and of course it hadn't been opened.'

There was soon to be a treat for all of us, and it would be hard to say which enjoyed it most, Arthur or I or the boys. As I opened the door to Arthur one evening he exclaimed, 'I've had a letter from Bourne!' 'Well,' said I, 'that's common enough, what is there to be excited about?' 'But it was posted in London. He and his wife and little girl are actually in England—landed yesterday—and are now at an hotel. I've told him to bring them here at once. We can put them up, can't we?'

Yes, indeed, there was room for all. Bourne was an old and dear friend, and I feared him not, but I was rather nervous of Mrs. Bourne, lest she should be too grand for our simple household. I learnt afterwards that she was nervous of me lest I should be clever. Both illusions were dispelled at our first meal, for as she helped me place the children round the table and dispense the food, I announced, 'Now if anybody wants anything he must just scream.'

All lessons were discarded at once. The youngest boy had been engaged in copying out the national anthem, and left it at the stage of 'Long live our nob'. Hilda, the little girl, came in age near the younger boys. She was an only child, brought up very carefully and properly, and her delight was intense when she found that she could get as muddy and untidy as she liked, without any reprimand. She was astonished, too, that bruises and grazed knees had no remedies applied, but were expected to heal up of themselves. This taste of freedom was intoxicating to her. When the boys asked her if she was a South African native she denied it a little indignantly, but had to admit that she had been born there, and then the misunderstanding was cleared up. She was an eager listener to stories, and I remember how much she liked Tolstoi's *What Men Live By*.

The charge of the four children fell to me most of the time, for Mrs. Bourne had a great deal of shopping to do in London. Her husband had business of his own in town, and he used to take her up with him, deposit her in Swan & Edgar's or Peter Robinson's, or some similar emporium, with instructions to take a cab as soon as she came out to the next place she wanted to visit. Now she was a perfect stranger to London and was so completely dazed that she drove to the station to get back to Barnet as soon as she decently could. I soon gathered that all she experienced of a London street was the bit of pavement between the shop-door and the cab.

'The way to see London,' said I, 'is to walk about and press your nose against the window-panes, or get on the top of a bus. Let's all go up together to-morrow, and I'll show you how to enjoy it. What shop have you got to visit next?'

'I was recommended to a shop in St. Paul's Churchyard, but of course there must be some mistake. The idea of a shop in a churchyard!'

'There's nothing funny in that,' said I. 'There are lots of shops in it. You shall see.'

She and I and all the children had a grand prowl about the City, into St. Paul's and along the alleys and by the dignified hidden dwellings close by.

'You think shops in a churchyard are funny,' said I, 'what do you say to a church called St. Andrew's by the Wardrobe?'

By this time Mrs. Bourne was prepared for any oddity, and we went down Carter Lane to a little turning called Wardrobe Place where old trees are growing out of a paved yard, the remains of the garden of the ancient house called the King's Wardrobe. Then we went on to see St. Andrew's, and then to Blackfriars to see the river. And on the top of a bus back to King's Cross we saw no end of other things.

As their fathers went off to town after breakfast every day the children saw little of them till the week-end. But Arthur delighted Hilda by going to kiss her good-night; she seemed like his little daughter. She was tremendously impressed with his top hat—a thing to which she was quite unused.

We grown-ups had plenty of fun in the evenings, talking of old times, telling new stories, and arguing far into the night. Among all our good neighbours in Barnet there was no one of Bourne's mental calibre, and I could see how refreshing to Arthur was this first-rate talk with accompaniment of fire and pipe.

When Sunday came we set off for church. Feeling a little anxious as to how the vicar's 'practices' might strike Mrs. Bourne, I asked her whether the church in Capetown was a high one. 'Not very, I'm afraid,' she replied, and added more hopefully, 'but they are thinking of building a tower.' I had no more concern on this point. The children filed into our usual pew, and I felt proud of my increased family. I didn't notice that when the boys placed their hats neatly down in front of them Hilda followed suit and placed her little blue cap alongside. Presently the verger touched my arm and whispered, 'Is that a little girl? Would you ask her to put her hat on?' Obviously the Bournes were not great church-goers, and Hilda had some difficulty in keeping her end up when she was questioned by the eldest boy as to her favourite feast-day, her favourite psalm, her favourite hymn, and so on. She only knew of Christmas, of 'The Lord is my shepherd,' and 'Onward Christian soldiers,' but as these were quite a natural choice her ignorance of any others was not observed, and it is only lately that she has told me of how awkward she felt. When it came to putting together the puzzle of the English counties the boys were genuinely shocked at her not knowing any of them, not even Cornwall from Durham. She was too polite to retaliate with some searching questions about Africa. Indeed, she was perfectly happy to be told everything as they all rampaged about the house and garden and woods.

'What a darling little girl she is,' said Arthur to me when they had gone, 'how I wish that our boys were better behaved. I feel quite ashamed when I see other children so polite and obedient—their cousins, for instance, how good they are.'

'Yes, of course they are,' said I. 'When their favourite uncle comes to see them they are gracious hosts, and when they come here they are gracious guests. No father ever really sees other people's children. Let's hope they're naughty enough in the bosom of their own family.'

'Hope? Why should we hope they are naughty?'

'Well, if children always did exactly as they were told, were always unthinkingly obedient, how could the world advance? And how dull it would be. Tell me now, did you ever do anything really bad when you were a boy?'

'I often used to go blind with rage.'

'That's all right. It's better to have a temper to curb than to have none at all.'

'But sometimes it was ugly enough. Once, when Llewelyn was asked to a party and I wasn't, I filled his boots with water. It's nothing to laugh at, I've always been ashamed of it.'

'Anything else?'

'Well, once I played truant from our little school. Off I started to get a whole long time to myself fishing in our stream at Corris. It was just the day for it—fish rising beautifully, and I got some fine trout.'

I noticed as he spoke that his eyes were shining at the recollection of that day, and I added, 'There you are! An act of insubordination and a joy for ever.'